Shining
Through
James

*Living the Journey
That Doesn't
Make Sense*

A Five-Week Study

Deborah Presnell

GRACE
PUBLISHING

BROKEN ARROW, OK

For Information Contact
Grace Publishing
PO Box 1233
Broken Arrow, OK 74013

Cover Image: Depositphotos

Shining Through James Living the Journey That Doesn't Make Sense

ISBN 13: 978-1-60495-067-0

About Copyrights

For Carol Clark
My Fourth Grade Teacher

Who, upon learning of my faith in Jesus Christ, wrote me this note:

"To Debbie, as you therefore have received Christ Jesus the Lord, so walk with Him."

Colossians 2:6

In Christian love,

Mrs. Clark

April 27, 1972

And who, after participating in my online Bible study, wrote me another note:

"Much love to a gifted little girl all grown up."

April 9, 2020

Table of Contents

Welcome Friends 7

How to Use This Bible Study 9

Overview 11

Week 1: James Chapter 1

Day One: Devoted 13

Day Two: Perfect and Complete 18

Day Three: The Wisdom of Single-Minded Devotion 26

Day Four: Transformed 34

Day Five: New Faith ~ New Behaviors 42

Week 2: James Chapter 2

Day One: Love: It's Royal! 54

Day Two: Sin: Major, Minor, Everything in Between 61

Day Three: Compelled to Obey 68

Day Four: A Friend of God 77

Day Five: Leave It All Behind 83

Week 3: James Chapter 3

Day One: A Woman of Influence 94

Day Two: Under Control 101

Day Three: The Choice Is Ours 109

Day Four: The Double Life 117

Day Five: Biblical Wisdom 125

Week 4: James Chapter 4

Day One: God Is Faithful . . . Are We? 132

Day Two: Drawing Close 141

Day Three: Criticism Versus Reproof 150

Day Four: Who Decides? 159

Day Five: Oblivious 167

Week 5: James Chapter 5

Day One: Everlasting Treasures 175

Day Two: Patience 183

Day Three: I Swear (Not)! 194

Day Four: All Kinds of Sickness 199

Day Five: Let's Pray 209

How to Make a Decision for Christ 223

About the Author 225

Endnotes 227

Welcome Friends!

We're embarking on a five-week journey together through the book of James. It's a short book of five chapters. Some have referred to James as the "Proverbs of the New Testament" — because its powerful teachings and wisdom transform the lives of those who choose to live by these biblical principles.

Most Bible scholars agree that the author of the book of James is the half-brother of Jesus. As a teaching pastor and leader in the church, James wrote this letter to encourage and instruct Jews who had placed their faith in Jesus Christ and decided to follow Him as their Messiah.

But some of the Christ-followers — Christians — reverted to their worldly, disobedient behavior and sinful lifestyle. There were discrepancies about money. The words¡ from their mouths had become weapons they wielded against other Christians. Conflict abounded, which only fueled quarrels with one another. This discord flowed into the worship and organization of the church, causing friction and division. Spiritually, these Christians were immature, behaving like undisciplined children who couldn't get along.

These problems sound familiar.

James boldly, yet lovingly, admonished the Christ-followers to start behaving like Christians — Christians who courageously position themselves as a lighthouse on a hill shining the light in a dark world. So, he addressed true religion, faith, testing and trials, wisdom, and everyday conflict. He balanced his teaching with encouragement and practical ways to live the Christian faith. And this is what we need — fellowship with one another that brings support, accountability, and love within our Christian circle.

This raises the question — how is a Christ-follower expected to act? Matthew 5:16 tells us, *Let your light shine before men in such a way that they may see your good works, and glorify your Father who is in heaven.* Jesus is the truth and the light. To reflect the light, we'll need to cling to biblical principles. Physical growth is automatic, yet spiritual growth requires training and perseverance. As we journey through James together, we'll be challenged, convicted, and hungry for truth.

Get ready to delve deeper into your personal life. Be prepared for spiritual and emotional confrontation. When we see ourselves from God's perspective it makes His grace, mercy, and forgiveness so much more fantastic. We discover that we love this journey that doesn't always make sense to onlookers but is explainable because of God's presence in our lives.

Grab a friend or two — that's what I did. Our journey through life is better when shared with a community of close friends who provide accountability, insight, and encouragement. In fact, you'll hear my friends' unique perspectives at the end of each study.

Let's get started. The journey, complete with its joys and struggles, will be worth it.

How to Use This Study

Shining Through James is a five-week study designed to be used alone or with a small group. In addition to this book, you'll need a Bible and a pen or pencil. Scriptures primarily come from the New American Standard Bible (NASB), but when another version is used, it's noted. Keep in mind as you study that when a Bible version capitalizes the word LORD OR LORD, it is reflecting the Hebrew word Yahweh — the eternal I Am (from a root word meaning "to be," or eternal existence). When the word Lord is written with standard capitalization, it is personal, reflecting the Hebrew word Adonai, literally meaning "my Lord," (from a root word which suggests sovereignty, strength and power).[1]

The time you spend in each chapter will vary. You can complete a chapter in one sitting or complete it over several days.

Page nine provides an idea of the topics you will examine, explore, and apply. I encourage you to pray before beginning each study. Ask God to reveal what He wants you to see and learn. Be honest with God and yourself. Also on the overview page are four questions to reflect on through your time with God. These questions are listed at the end of each chapter.

Let the journey begin. Shine on!

Topics to be Discussed:

As you study each chapter, consider the following:

- What did God reveal about His character?

- How have you been challenged in a specific area of your life?

- How will you apply the passage to your daily routine?

- How is your faith being strengthened?

Generally speaking feeling joyful when we suffer, or loving the unlovable doesn't make sense. But at the end of this study, our lives will be different. And by the power of the Holy Spirit, we can love the journey that doesn't make sense.

Overview

Week 1 Chapter 1	Week 2 Chapter 2	Week 3 Chapter 3	Week 4 Chapter 4	Week 5 Chapter 5
Who is James?	Partiality	Teachers and preachers	God's jealousy	Ungodly rich
Humility	Favoritism	Scribes / Pharisees	Spiritual adultery	Treasure
Servanthood	Judging others	Hidden sin	Conforming to the world's standards	Patience
Devotion	Love	Our speech	Friendship with the world	Swearing
Endurance	Evidence of faith	Rudder / bit / spark	Walking with God	Suffering
Spiritual maturity	Sin	Tiny tools	Humility	Christian character
Perfect & Complete	Forgiveness	The Heart's condition	Pride	Worship
Trials / Adversity	Mercy	The tongue	Submission	Emotional, physical, mental, spiritual sickness
Joy	Works vs. Faith	Foul language	Confession	Healing
Perseverance	Genuine faith	Abusive language	Criticism	Sin
Wisdom	Boundaries	Gossip	Biblical accountability	Rest
Single-mindedness	Abraham, God's friend	Pleasant words	Confrontation	Confession
Wealth	Rahab	Bless God	Judgment	Confrontation
Temptation	God's love	Double-mindedness	Making decisions	Praying for others
Anger	Taking risks	Godly wisdom	Planning ahead	Persistence
Doer vs. Hearer	The law	Earthly wisdom	God's will	Effective prayer
	The royal law		Using time wisely	When God hears
	The law of liberty		A sin of omission	Elijah
	Past, present, future		A sin of commission	Job
	Saved by grace			
	Compelled to obey			

Faith and obedience are traveling companions
heading to the same destination
of pleasing and glorifying the Lord.

Charles Stanley

Week 1, Day 1

Devoted

Read James 1:1:

James, a bond-servant of God and of the Lord Jesus Christ, to the twelve tribes who are dispersed abroad: Greetings.

*I*f anyone could have elevated his relationship with Jesus — flaunting to other Christ-followers — James, the younger half-brother of Jesus, could have. Can you imagine? "Yeah, the Son of Almighty God . . . He's my brother."

Based on what we know directly or indirectly about families, it's plausible the boys watched their father create furniture from wood or stone, shared a cookie, or snuggled under a wool blanket while looking at the stars. Perhaps Jesus taught James to fish.

But as the boys became men their early bond may have become detached; their relationship, warped in emotional conflict.

John 7:5 tells us that James didn't believe Jesus was the prophesied Messiah. None of Jesus' siblings did. If James didn't believe Jesus was the Savior, he might have thought his brother was crazy. Perhaps James was embarrassed by the things Jesus did and said, prompting snide remarks, harsh criticisms, and laughter behind His back — or to His face. Maybe James was jealous of his parents' relationship with Jesus — the perfect child with extraordinary moral character — invoking sibling resentment.

But then the miracle of the resurrection happened, and a radical transformation occurred in James' life. He became a devoted believer — a Christ-follower. He saw Jesus from a different perspective — that of the Savior. Perhaps he was ashamed of the way he had treated his brother when they lived in the same house. Or maybe he was regretful that he hadn't seen the truth all along.

Scripture doesn't go into the private details surrounding James' sentiments, but we do know one thing: His gratitude and humility compelled him to serve God and dedicate himself to leading the church. He shone with a bright light, radiating his love for Jesus. Now, that's a powerful transformation.

For James to identify himself as Jesus' brother would've been the truth, yet, James intentionally separated himself on the relational level and introduced himself as a *bond-servant* of God.

Becoming a servant doesn't sound glamorous in the least. Why would anyone want to do that? We like the freedom to do as we please . . . until our freedom takes us down the wrong path.

The Greek word for bond-servant is *doulos*. It means a servant who gives himself up to advance the cause or service of another.[2]

Why do you think James characterized his relationship as Jesus' bond-servant and not His relative?

In Romans 6:22 we read: *But now being made free from sin, and become servants to God, ye have your fruit unto holiness, and the end everlasting life* (KJV). How does becoming a servant of God make us truly free?

We're all enslaved or devoted to something or someone — and that someone might be ourself. Is there anything preventing you from being free and totally devoted to Jesus with your whole heart?

James' gratitude compelled him to embrace servanthood. He reflected on Jesus' selfless behavior and genuine love. He understood the seriousness and importance of the cross and resurrection. And it changed his life. James took a new path.

What about you? Are you, like James — who in his youth didn't believe Jesus — still struggling with unbelief?

If you've embraced faith in God, did you come to Him out of fear, then after receiving a secure place in heaven, choose your own journey and leave God out?

Or, as James did when he grew to be a man, have you fully and gratefully embraced the cross and its power to change you and make you free?

Are you willing to become a servant? If not, what frightens you? What holds you back?

In what ways do you grasp the depth of God's love and mercy?

Maybe you have family members who don't believe Jesus is the Savior. How does the sibling relationship of Jesus and James give you hope?

When gratitude compels us to servanthood, we're destined to becoming perfect and complete. We'll discuss this in the next chapter.

Notes

It doesn't make sense that by becoming a servant, we reflect freedom. But when the Holy Spirit opens our minds and hearts to comprehend the significance of the cross, gratitude compels us to serve.

Prayer

God, help me know

- what to do.
- what to say.
- what to think.
- where to go.

For Reflection

What did God reveal about His character?

How have you been challenged in a specific area of your life?

How will you apply the passage to your daily routine?

How is your faith being strengthened?

Godly Friends Chime In

JUDY says, "James had the truth right in front of him, even in his own house, and yet he didn't see it. How often is the truth right in front of me, and I just don't see it? Oh, God, give us magnifiers to see Your truth!"

LORIE chimes in, "As I read this study this morning, the words came alive. At the end of last year, I began to pray and ask God to show me areas in my life I needed to change. He spoke, *No other gods before God.* I started journaling after my devotion time, and He revealed something that I needed to let go of and to focus on Him. I cannot be a true servant of Christ if I focus on me and continue to be pulled in every direction. All that I do should be for the glory of God. It's not about me but Christ who lives in me."

SAVANNAH agrees. "It's crystal clear to me that servanthood is self-denial and that is where all the freedom is, isn't it? When the focus is completely off of me, I am relieved of such weight!"

Perfect and Complete

Read James 1:2–4:

> *Consider it all joy, my brethren, when you encounter various trials, knowing that the testing of your faith produces endurance. And let endurance have its perfect result, so that you may be perfect and complete, lacking in nothing.*

> I couldn't have imagined that six months after responding to God's call to write and teach a Bible study on "joy while suffering," I'd be writing it from the third floor of a cancer center. My exploration through the book of James was about to get real.
>
> Yep. Cancer.
>
> Like an uninvited hitchhiker, cancer burst onto my husband's path . . . and mine.
>
> For sure, we were blindsided by our medical emergency, but we had to put our heads together, become proactive, and deal with the unthinkable — this unexpected, unforeseen, unwanted distraction. I wondered how I could continue to shine.

*E*vents like this have different names — *trial, affliction, trouble, suffering,* or *adversity.* Broken relationships, major decisions, disappointments, and health issues are also trials. Serving Jesus with a heart of gratitude doesn't exempt us from troubles. Reread James 1:2 and fill in the missing word:

Consider it all joy _____ *you suffer various trials.* Not *if.* We can anticipate trials during our lifetime.

What personal trial are you currently suffering? If you're not in a trial now, describe a past trial.

John 16:33 tells us this: *In this world you will have tribulation.* What is your gut reaction to this reality?

Is it too much to expect to experience joy during trials? Explain why or why not.

Hebrews 2:9 tells us that Jesus suffered *for a little while* so that all could receive salvation. He submitted to an excruciating death. How does Jesus' agonizing pain for a short amount of time for a life-changing outcome, give you hope?

The KJV uses the term *divers temptation* — or diverse temptations — in place of the term *trials* in James 1:2. We may view temptation as coming from the devil as he tempts us to do what we think will bring us pleasure. But a person can also be tempted to worry, to fear, or to doubt God's love — definitely not a pleasurable disposition.[3]

The New Testament uses three Greek words for trials:

Dokimion[4]   Is used when proving one's faith is genuine. It's what's found in us after we are tested.

Purosis[5]   Is used when we go through the fires of suffering for the purpose of refining one's character.

Peirasmos[6]   Is used when God is testing our commitment. Will we remain faithful to Him or we will fall into temptation and sin?

Trials have many and varying purposes. Using the Greek meanings, can you determine the purpose of the trial you described on the previous page? Are you able to see the end yet?

King David was familiar with all kinds of trials, for different reasons, and with varying outcomes. Read Psalm 69:1–2. David used the term *mire* to describe his pain and trouble. (As used here, it means a state of difficulty, distress, or embarrassment from which it is hard to extricate oneself.) How would you describe the various emotions that accompanied any of your trials?

In 2 Corinthians 4:8–9 Paul wrote: *We are afflicted in every way, but not crushed; perplexed, but not despairing; persecuted, but not forsaken; struck down, but not destroyed.*

We can apply this truth to what's afflicting us by filling in these blanks.

I am afflicted by_____ but I'm not _____;

I feel _____ but not _____;

persecuted by _____ but I am not_____;

taken by surprise in_____ but_____.

Paul continued in 2 Corinthians 4:16–17: *We do not lose heart, but though our outer man is decaying, yet our inner man is being renewed day by day. For momentary, light affliction is producing for us an eternal weight of glory far beyond all comparison.*

How does *momentary* encourage you?

Peter, a close friend of James and a fellow servant of Jesus Christ, wrote: *In this you greatly rejoice, even though now for a little while, if necessary, you have been distressed by various trials, so that the proof of your faith, being more precious than gold which is perishable, even though tested by fire, may be found to result in praise and glory and honor at the revelation of Jesus Christ* (1 Peter 1:6–7).

Are you distressed? Cry out to God. Tell Him the pain feels too hard or unfair. That's what David did. His example of transparency helps us feel less alone. Throughout the Psalms, David ranted, questioned, and cried out. Yet, in predictable fashion, he habitually praised God too. Again and again David was healed, restored, and strengthened. His faith was purified — like gold refined by fire.

In what ways are you like David?

Do you give equal time to ranting and praising?

While we're suffering for a little while, James and Peter tell us to rejoice. If you open a thesaurus to synonyms for *rejoice,* you won't find "trials" there — because they're opposites. In fact, to be able to experience joy during trials is contrary to our human thinking.

The Greek word for joy is *chara,* which means to "rejoice or delight in; to experience God's grace."[7] Joy isn't being happy. Joy comes from experiencing God's grace. Joy occurs naturally, perhaps unexpectedly, when our spiritual eyes remain focused on Him — in dependence, humility, servanthood, and delight.

Take a look at the synonyms for joy: bubbly, lighthearted, good humored. Joy is the result of clinging to God's truth. Joy is finding contentment in Him despite the circumstances. Contentment in God enables a person to exude an optimistic, hopeful attitude. People from all cultures and religions notice this kind of mind-set.

James says to "consider it joy" during trials. The *New King James Version* uses the word "count" in place of "consider." *Merriam Webster's Dictionary* defines *count* as "naming, or tallying and reckoning; to consider and account oneself lucky."[8]

While in the midst of a trial, have you been able to tally up the occurrences of genuine joy? If so, write about it. If not, what kept you from having joy?

To help us have joy while suffering, we must focus on the truth that trials:

- won't last forever.
- aid in refinement.
- help us find contentment with God.
- make us perfect and complete.

Return to our passage in James 1:2–4. Circle the words "perfect and complete." The Greek word for perfection, *teleios*, means "completeness."[9] Perfect faith in God makes us completely mature spiritually. To complete the process, we'll need endurance.

Read Romans 5:3–4. Fill in the missing words in this paraphrased statement:

Tribulations brings about _____ which produces _____ which produces _____.

In our passage today, James used the word *endurance* — steadfastness or perseverance. Christ-followers gain additional endurance

with each trial, which produces a deeper, stronger level of faith.
Endurance is increased when we trust God for a good outcome.

So, as my husband and I embarked on the cancer journey I wondered, *God, when You told me to write a Bible study on joy during suffering, was it to prepare me for this sickness? Or would this experience give me a new perspective?* It didn't matter which came first. They were both here.

And then it happened.

I heard the most surprising and beautiful words I had ever heard. Alan and I were sitting on the sofa watching TV when he reached over to me, touched my hand and said, "I have something to say."

"Okay," I said.

"I have so much joy right now," he said. "I guess this doesn't make sense coming from a man with cancer." He chuckled. "But I do. In fact, I may have the most joy I've ever had in my whole life."

Tears puddled in my eyes, then gently coursed down my face.

"When they show I'm cancer free, I'll fall prostrate on the floor and praise God. Well, regardless of what happens . . . I'll fall prostrate and praise God."

Alan and I are physically weary, yet spiritually strong; overwhelmed, yet hopeful; sad at the occurrence of cancer, yet simultaneously joyful.

Explainable joy. Joy that comes from abiding in the presence of the Lord.

The theme of Psalm 91 is the perilous pestilence — the dangerous or unsafe destruction or disease — that God delivers us from (v. 3 NKJV) when we dwell in the presence of God. Dwelling — living — in His presence, devoted to God. This is how we survive sorrow and experience simultaneous joy.

Author and theologian Charles Spurgeon wrote in his devotional *Morning and Evening,* "In the earth I wander, but in God I dwell in a quiet habitation."[10]

When we dwell with God, rejoice in hope, persevere in tribulation, and are devoted to prayer (Romans 12:12), we're becoming perfect and complete.

Prayer

God, help me know:

- what to do
- what to say
- what to think
- where to go

For Reflection

What did God reveal about His character?

How have you been challenged in a specific area of your life?

How will you apply the passage to your daily routine?

How is your faith being strengthened?

Godly Friends Chime In

SHERRY opens up. "There have been many tribulations, and most of them have been health related. When a new problem arises, I just say, 'Here we go growing again.' Sometimes the faith growth is substantial, while others are baby steps. The trial of my autoimmune disease has already lasted 15 years. I've been on the mountaintop of faith and in the valley, crying out just as David did. But through it all, God has been faithful, and I've never struggled alone. In fact, He has brought joy despite my circumstances."

CAROL joins the conversation. "The Lord has allowed a few big trials to come into my life over the years. Do I thank Him for the trials while I'm in the midst of them? No, but I have learned to rejoice in the blessings (no matter how small) that He supplies throughout the trial. Some would have been overlooked, taken for granted, or dismissed as good luck, but because of the circumstances, I realized God was giving me golden nuggets of happiness and joy to hold on to. God was showing me that He was and is with me each step of the way. Now, as I look back upon the trials, I thank Him for taking me through and never leaving me to myself. How do I know that He was always with me? He gave me tidbits of joy — some small others large — and He continues to provide blessings along life's journey."

JUDY admits, "This passage brings back so many memories. I have also experienced the joy that comes from placing my burdens at the feet of Jesus (sometimes over and over again), only to feel the great love He has for me and to know that He is sufficient to carry the trials of this life. Truly, I don't think I could ever experience His love without leaning on Him during those dark times. Reflecting on this makes me feel instant joy!"

Week 1, Day 3

The Wisdom of Single-Minded Devotion

Read James 1:5–8:

> *If any of you lacks wisdom, let him ask of God, who gives to all generously and without reproach, and it will be given to him. But he must ask in faith without any doubting, for the one who doubts is like the surf of the sea, driven and tossed by the wind. For that man ought not to expect that he will receive anything from the Lord, being a double-minded man, unstable in all his ways.*

I enjoy deep conversations with the fourth graders I sometimes teach. I say deep because Mason's response to the question, "What do you think wisdom is?" took me by surprise.

"Wisdom," he said, "comes from your experience in the world and how you use it to impact people in good ways." I guess he noticed my surprise. He gave me a sheepish grin. Later that day, I compared the different definitions for wisdom in a number of dictionaries and discovered that Mason's definition is similar to those of Bible scholars, in particularly, author and Bible commentator, Warren Wiersbe. He writes, "Knowledge enables us to take things apart, but wisdom enables us to put things together and relate truth to daily life."[11] In essence, the wisdom of God enables us to glow with the truth of God — burnished into our heart.

The Free Dictionary defines knowledge and wisdom this way:

- Knowledge is "information gained through experience, reasoning, or acquaintance."
- Wisdom is "the ability to discern or judge what is true, right, or lasting."[12]

The Greek word for wisdom is *sophia*. It means having the "ability to judge correctly and to follow the best course of action, based on knowledge and understanding."[13]

Spurgeon wrote, "Wisdom is the right use of knowledge. To know is not to be wise. Many men [and women] know a great deal, and are all the greater fools for it. There is no fool so great a fool as a knowing fool. But to know how to use knowledge is to have wisdom."[14]

What do you think Spurgeon meant by, "To know is not to be wise?"

A person can have knowledge without having wisdom. But one cannot have wisdom without having knowledge. For example, one can know how to operate a computer, but wisdom is knowing when to keep it locked and which sites to block.

Recall James 1:5. Who is eligible to receive wisdom? Circle or make note of the phrase, *any of you* in the first sentence. Do you sometimes think there are others who are more deserving of God's wisdom than you? Why or why not?

Do you sometimes feel that *any of* you means *everyone but you*? If so, explain.

When, if ever, have you asked for wisdom but felt like you received confusion?

First Corinthians 14:33 tells us *God is not a God of confusion.* In the context of seeking direction, God is the Giver of three things. According to Proverbs 2:6, what three things does God give?

So then, if God is willing to give, *when* and *how* does a person receive it?

There's an axiom that the gray hair on older women is a symbol of wisdom. But age and spiritual maturity aren't necessarily synonymous. Just because a woman is older, doesn't make her wiser; spending time with God each day is how we become spiritually mature and wise. In this way, a younger Christian woman can be spiritually wiser than her unbelieving elder. Any woman who chooses to leave God out of her daily life remains unchanged by Him. Birthdays don't make us wise — a relationship with Jesus does.

When James instructed his brothers and sisters in Christ to ask God for wisdom, he knew that achieving such spiritual insight was obtainable. Jesus revealed this truth. Read Matthew 7:7 and fill in the missing words.

_____ *and it will be* _____ *to you;* _____ *and you will find;* _____ *and it will be opened to you.*

Perhaps receiving wisdom sounds like a glorious endeavor. Yet, wisdom is simple to obtain. Simple . . . because all we need to do is ask.

I recall when I urgently needed to make a vital decision regarding my mom's health care and rehabilitation options. With only days until decision time, I was overwhelmed with the choices — and the fear of making the wrong one. On a Sunday night, my heart called out to God:

"I need wisdom to know what to do! I boldly come before the throne of grace asking for wisdom that You said You'd give. I'm going to pray intentionally and with purpose until You give me an answer. But more than that, You must also provide my mom with the same wisdom so we're in complete agreement. And we must have it now."

My prayer continued for two days. Then I visited my mom in the hospital. After praying together, Mom smiled and said, "Last night I had a dream. I was in a room with a large picture window. Fall flowers were growing in the garden, and I could see birds eating at the feeders. I commented to the nurse that my daughter would come decorate the sterile-looking room and make it more attractive."

My mom looked into my eyes and said that God was showing her where she needed to go. God gave both my mother and me the wisdom to make the right choice. We hugged and cried tears of joy. The wisdom God provided filled us with peace.

What do you need specific wisdom for?

Previously I asked when and how a person gets wisdom. We learned wisdom is given when we seek and cultivate a relationship with God. Job identified where we won't find wisdom. Read what Job 28:12–15 says: *"Where can wisdom be found? And where is the place of understanding? Man does not know its value, nor is it found in the land of the living. The deep says, 'It is not in me'; and the sea says, 'It is not with me.' Pure gold cannot be given in exchange for it, nor can silver be weighed as its price."*

Wisdom is not found in _____ or the
_____ and _____ and
_____ can't be exchanged for it.

Wisdom is more valuable and precious than pure silver or gold.

Persevere. Daily seek God. The wisdom you gain will impede double-mindedness. That word, *double-minded,* comes from the Greek word *dipsuchos* and only occurs in the book of James. Double-minded describes a person with two minds or souls,[15] someone who is unstable, unsteady, and wavering in character and allows circumstances and feelings to determine the goodness and faithfulness of God.

When have you allowed your situation to determine your conclusions about God?

The hypocrisy of wavering emotions creates an inner struggle. Can you relate to this confusing state between having faith one moment and unbelief the next? If so, how?

The apostle Peter could relate. Read Matthew 14:22–33. Jesus commanded Peter to leave the boat and walk to Him on water. What happened first?

What do you think distracted Peter?

What happened when Peter took his eyes off Jesus?

When Peter focused on Jesus, his faith abounded and enabled him to obey. But when his gaze was diverted to the challenge and complexity of his surroundings, fear welled up, doubt crept in, and he began to sink — literally and figuratively.

Doubt can't exist where belief lives; fear can't triumph where peace is present. Single-mindedness — devotion to God alone — leads to spiritual wisdom.

Prayer

God, help me know

- what to do.
- what to say.
- what to think.
- where to go.

It doesn't make sense that we can glow with the wisdom of God, but gratitude, servanthood, and focused devotion make wisdom possible.

For Reflection

What did God reveal about His character?

How have you been challenged in a specific area of your life?

How will you apply the passage to your daily routine?

How is your faith being strengthened?

Godly Friends Chime In

SAVANNAH, fired up, says, "I always have it in the forefront of my mind that my feelings are fickle. But God's Word is not. It should be the final authority of my life. Asking God for wisdom means that we search His Word. It means we beat the drums of daily devotion!"

JAN shares, "When I was getting ready to move to Tennessee I was praying and asking God for wisdom. Should I do this or should I not? The day I got an offer from someone to buy my house in North Carolina was actually very confusing. I remember praying and asking God again if this is what He wanted me to do. Then I asked Him to show me. When I opened the contract the date that the buyers wanted to close was the exact date when my magazine goes to press. As the editor of a monthly magazine I am incredibly busy right up until that deadline. But on that morning when the magazine goes to press, I have several days with time to do other things I enjoy — and this includes time to move to a new state. Only God knew that day was the perfect day. After that I felt complete peace that this was the right move."

Week 1, Day 4

Transformed

Read James 1:9–18:

> *The brother of humble circumstances is to glory in his high position; and the rich man is to glory in his humiliation, because like flowering grass he will pass away. For the sun rises with a scorching wind and withers the grass; and its flower falls off and the beauty of its appearance is destroyed; so too the rich man in the midst of his pursuits will fade away. Blessed is a man who perseveres under trial; for once he has been approved, he will receive the crown of life which the Lord has promised to those who love Him. Let no one say when he is tempted, "I am being tempted by God"; for God cannot be tempted by evil, and He Himself does not tempt anyone. But each one is tempted when he is carried away and enticed by his own lust. Then when lust has conceived, it gives birth to sin; and when sin is accomplished, it brings forth death. Do not be deceived, my beloved brethren. Every good thing given and every perfect gift is from above, coming down from the Father of lights, with whom there is no variation or shifting shadow. In the exercise of His will He brought us forth by the word of truth, so that we would be a kind of first fruits among His creatures.*

*D*o you recall when frost blanketed the ground and killed the remaining summer flowers and paused the growth of grass? Why do you think that James compares a rich man to a withering flower?

For starters, let's define what it means to wither. *Webster's* defines withering as "becoming dry and shriveled; losing vitality, force or freshness."[16] The Greek word for withering, *xeraino*, means to "waste away."[17]

Earthly riches, trials, and temptation, may appear to be unrelated, but withering connects them. How so?

Without God, our natural selfish tendencies lure us to all manners of evil. Without God, we'd wither in the agony of a trial and our light would grow dim. And without God, the pull on us to surrender to temptation would destroy us.

However, God made a way for us to stay vital. In Psalm 1:1–3 we read: *How blessed is the man who does not walk in the counsel of the wicked, nor stand in the path of sinners, nor sit in the seat of scoffers! But his delight is in the law of the LORD, and in His law he meditates day and night. He will be like a tree firmly planted by streams of water, which yields its fruit in its season and its leaf does not wither; and in whatever he does, he prospers.*

According to the above verse, what two things make a person vital, fresh, and blessed?

That's a life-changing revelation.

We're firmly rooted, steadfast in trials, able to bear fruit, boldly resist temptation, and accept testing as teachable moments, when we love God's Word and meditate on it.

In fact, *what* we pursue, *how* we endure trials, our *response* to temptation, and what we believe about God's goodness are directly linked to the time we devote to God's Word and our decision to obey His instruction. We'll either wither, dry up, and waste away, or we'll stay fresh, vital, and strong. Staying fresh or drying up depends on what we choose to think about. Romans 12:2 tells us: *Do not be conformed to this world, but be transformed by the renewing of your mind.*

Being transformed changes our minds and attitudes toward:

- riches
- trials
- temptation versus testing
- God's goodness

When God transforms our mind, we begin to see His perspective and, as a result, our natural strivings, inclinations, and desires align with God's purpose for us.

Saul changed his mind and was dramatically transformed.

Saul was a devoted Jewish leader — zealous for Hebrew religious tradition — who proudly ascribed to Jewish law. He hated Christ-followers and believed they were disloyal to God. He partnered with the high priest to murder them. Galatians 1:13 tells us that Saul tried to destroy Christianity.

But when God showed up on the Damascus Road, He had Saul's full attention. While blinded for three days, Saul began to spiritually see the truth. When Saul began preaching instead of persecuting, the Jews were shocked. They sought to have him killed.

God transformed Saul's life in a powerful way. Instead of trying to kill the gospel, he became an instrument to propel it. Everything about his life changed — including his name. Saul became the apostle Paul. (See Acts 9.)

This same transformation is available to us. In 2 Corinthians 5:17 we read this: *If anyone is in Christ, he is a new creature; the old things passed away; behold, new things have come.*

What about you? In what ways do you demonstrate your new life? (If you haven't accepted God's gift of salvation yet, see page 223.)

What behaviors have you released?

How has God transformed your attitude?

James begins with comparing the rich man to a withering flower not because wealth in and of itself is sinful but because the desire for earthly pleasures and pursuits takes our eyes off of God and puts them on ourselves and what we desire. Colossians 3:1–2 says: *Since, then, you have been raised with Christ, set your hearts on things above, where Christ is, seated at the right hand of God. Set your minds on things above, not on earthly things.*

Philippians 4:8 tells us what to set our mind on so that transformation can take place. What are we to think about?

Depending on your Bible version, you may read in Philippians 4:8, *meditate, fix, think about, dwell.* While fixing our mind of heavenly pursuits — those that last for eternity — we'll be able to resist giving in to earthly pleasures before they lead us into full-blown sin.

Think back to your school days. What was the teacher's purpose in giving you a test?

Your teacher gave you a test to find out the quality of what you know, or what you're about, or what you're thinking. God tests his followers, not to discover what they know, but for the purpose of her growth in perseverance, endurance, spiritual maturity, transformation, and refinement.

God's refinement process is the same that goldsmiths and silversmiths use to refine their ores. After years of being squeezed under the pressure of the earth, the rock is broken and heated until impurities, called dross, come to the surface. The refiner removes the dross, leaving behind gold and silver or a sparkling diamond. The silversmith knows his work with the silver is completed when he can look into his work and see his image. God's refinement occurs in the heat of adversity. During this time, our impurities bubble up to the surface, where God removes them, and leaves us transformed into the image of Christ.

Contrast testing with temptation. *Encyclopedia.com* defines *tempt* in reference to the Bible as "a trial in which man has a free choice of being faithful or unfaithful to God."[18] But God does not tempt us. He tests us for the purpose of transformation.

The refining process may not feel like God is good. But the end result will be good because anything good is from God — anything that we can grasp or experience like a beautiful sunrise, an unexpected paycheck, emotional healing, or a good meal. But God is also good in ways we might not have imagined, like the things we know nothing about because God intervened and stopped a disaster from coming and prevented what might have been.

In the middle of a trial may not feel like God is good, but when He's teaching us to remain steadfast and humbly dependent on Him, the relationship that ensues is better than anything this world can offer.

> Cancer treatments continued as my husband headed back to work. At one point he said, "I wish I knew if the treatment was going to be a success by the end of the year."
>
> I responded, "But if we knew the outcome would be good and that healing would come, would we still run to God every day in desperation? Would we still lean on Him in the way we are now?"
>
> "Maybe not," he agreed.
>
> "As crazy as this might sound, the not-knowing keeps us close and dependent on God — which is changing our lives way beyond the cancer journey. What a gift to be invited into a relationship with the heavenly Father and be totally dependent on Him with the gift of 'not knowing,'" I responded.

Romans 8:28 tells us *God causes all things to work together for good to those who love God, to those who are called according to His purpose.* This verse isn't implying that all things are good — because they're not. But collectively, God takes the most challenging and arduous situations and produces the right outcome.

Do you believe God is good? Why or why not?

May God transform our thoughts today about pursuing and spending money, staying strong in trials, being courageous in testing, and believing God is good.

Notes

It doesn't make sense that we can be a vital, strong, shining light when withering situations arise, but because we love and meditate on God's Word, God transforms our minds and our lives are shaped into the likeness of Christ.

Prayer

God, help me know

- what to do.
- what to say.
- what to think.
- where to go.

For Reflection

What did God reveal about His character?

How have you been challenged in a specific area of your life?

How will you apply the passage to your daily routine?

How is your faith being strengthened?

Godly Friends Chime In

SAVANNAH says, "Lord . . . what are you trying to teach me in regard to money and trials? I can appreciate a good chipping away of my character. I'm reminded of God's ability to provide despite what we think we need or when we think we don't have enough. Lord, give me what I need and if I don't have it, it's because you say I don't need it. Things of this world will never satisfy me. Only You can."

SHERRY joins the conversation. "The joy that accompanies a trial is watching God transform us . . . not watching others suffer."

ELEANOR shares, "Trials are never easy, but the outcome is always for His glory! I often use the phrase, 'ouch God,' when it hurts. But He always holds my hand and walks me through it. He wants us to be vital and not wither. I believe we can share our painful trials with someone who is going through the same thing. I could not get through the day without Him. I love how He's in the smallest little things and the huge things too! Also, with money, my greatest joy is in giving it away! I didn't mean to ramble . . . I just get so excited when I think about how good He is."

CAROL responds, "I remember when my husband said we should start tithing. We prayed because even knowing it was the right thing to do, we weren't sure our bills could be paid and stretch far enough to tithe. But we made the commitment. Each monthly payday, the tithe was the first check we wrote. Praise the Lord . . . our money stretched more each month! The Lord blessed us with contentment that only comes from doing what you know is right in the Lord. We knew what to do because we meditated on His Word."

Week 1, Day 5

New Faith ~ New Behaviors

Read James 1:19–27:

This you know, my beloved brethren. But everyone must be quick to hear, slow to speak and slow to anger; for the anger of man does not achieve the righteousness of God. Therefore, putting aside all filthiness and all that remains of wickedness, in humility receive the word implanted, which is able to save your souls. But prove yourselves doers of the word, and not merely hearers who delude themselves. For if anyone is a hearer of the word and not a doer, he is like a man who looks at his natural face in a mirror; for once he has looked at himself and gone away, he has immediately forgotten what kind of person he was. But one who looks intently at the perfect law, the law of liberty, and abides by it, not having become a forgetful hearer but an effectual doer, this man will be blessed in what he does. If anyone thinks himself to be religious, and yet does not bridle his tongue but deceives his own heart, this man's religion is worthless. Pure and undefiled religion in the sight of our God and Father is this: to visit orphans and widows in their distress, and to keep oneself unstained by the world.

An article from the Mayo Clinic reports, "Anger is a normal and even healthy emotion — but it's important to deal with it in a positive way. Uncontrolled anger can take a toll on both your health and your relationships."

The article went on to describe ten ways for a person to harness their anger. "*Think before you speak.* In the heat of the moment, it's easy to say something you'll later regret. *Take a few moments* to collect your thoughts before saying anything — and allow others involved in the situation to do the same."[19] (emphasis, mine.)

Truth. Yet, I rolled my eyes and smirked. *This* is what makes me angry — when others take credit for something God said.

The Matthew Henry Commentary, which has been one of the most widely used Bible commentaries for over 300 years, explains the ramification of anger in religious debate. "The worst thing we can bring to a religious controversy," Henry wrote, "is anger."[20] James implored Christ-followers to listen patiently in religious debate and then respond in truth, but without rage.

Unleashed, untimely, or inappropriate anger in a controversial conversation about religious practices, nonessentials, or legalism, hampers the message of the gospel, and damages all kinds of relationships in general. Perhaps we've justified our angry outbursts as part of our genetic makeup, but unlike blue eyes that can't be changed, anger can be controlled, even if we grew up in an angry environment where an angry response was deemed acceptable.

Reread James 1:20 and fill in the blank:

Anger does not _____
_____.

Are you prone to angry outbursts? If so, what sets you off? What strategies do you use to calm yourself?

If anger doesn't have its grip on you, have you ever been the recipient or been within earshot of another person's explosion? If yes, how did it make you feel?

Look further at God's Word. Match the Scriptures to their reference.

____	*Proverbs 14:17*	a. *Do not be eager in your heart to be angry, for anger resides in the bosom of fools.*
____	*Proverbs 16:32*	b. *A quick-tempered man acts foolishly, and a man of evil devices is hated.*
____	*Ecclesiastes 7:9*	c. *He who is slow to anger is better than the mighty, and he who rules his spirit, than he who captures a city.*
____	*Ephesians 4:31*	d. *Let all bitterness and wrath and anger and clamor and slander be put away from you, along with all malice.*
____	*Colossians 3:8*	e. *But now you also, put them all aside: anger, wrath, malice, slander, and abusive speech from your mouth.*

Often anger manifests through words.

Read Proverbs 17:27. [She] *who restrains [her] lips is* _____.

Hurtful words aren't always spoken in anger either. Maybe you can recall being on the receiving end of gossip, harsh criticism, hasty words, or slander.

James admonished his fellow Christ-followers to not only put aside their anger but also get rid of filthiness and wickedness. Wickedness, as defines in the *New King James Study Bible,* is "any habits, thoughts, or actions that remain from the old life of sin."[21] As Christians, our new life should be characterized with new behaviors. The Holy Spirit, who lives with us, removes old, sinful habits. Reread Colossians 3:8 (above). What do we need to get rid of?

Do any of these actions or attitudes surface on a regular basis? If so, which ones?

Some of James' readers returned to their old life of sin. What analogy did he use to lovingly admonish them? (vv.23–24)

How does the mirror analogy reflect what we sometimes do when reading the Bible?

On a scale of 1–10, with 10 being the highest, to what degree do you strive to live by Biblical principles?

   1   2   3   4   5   6   7   8   9   10

If you think living by Biblical principles seems too hard, you're right — if you're attempting it on your own. God knew this, so He gave us the gift of the Holy Spirit to empower us. His presence makes all things possible.

Reread James 1:26. When is a person deceived?

The Greek word for deceived, *dolioo*, means "using bait to pull someone in; to deceive, preying on people who are blinded by their own bitterness, greed or lust; 'easy prey' to ensnare."[22] On the previous page, we read what Colossians 3:8 told us to put away. To guard against deception, read Colossians 3:12–15. List what the Holy Spirit will help us put on.

Recall Romans 12:2: **Do not be conformed to this world, but be transformed by the renewing of your mind.** James reiterates Paul's point to not conform to our culture's expectations or beliefs. We must allow God to transform our thought patterns. Below, describe how we can be untouched by deceptive beliefs, yet make a difference.

At Work

At Play

At Home

To remain unspotted by our culture's dark, false beliefs, we'll need the implanted Word. Some Bible translations use the word *planted* (NIV), or *engrafted* (KJV) in verse 21. Synonyms for implanted are *rooted, inserted, established,* or *embedded.* Engrafted is a medical term that describes the procedure of surgically transplanting living tissue from one part of an individual to another part for its adhesion and growth.[23]

When a malignant melanoma emerged as a tumor in my husband's foot, the tumor was removed, yet he required reconstructive surgery and a skin graft. The doctor removed skin from one area of the body and grafted it — sewed it — onto the area that was wounded and useless. This graft served as protection and brought new life to the damaged area, allowing my husband's foot to function.

Similarly, to engraft Scripture means the living Word of God is firmly established in our heart, making us spiritually alive, able to thrive, and live victoriously. What do you think would happen if people had God's Word engrafted on their hearts?

What impact would this have on our neighborhoods, cities, states, and nation?

There's more good news, too. Romans 11:23–24 tells us we're grafted into God's family. What is the implication?

Engrafted Scripture enables us to produce spiritual fruit. Read Galatians 5:22 and list nine evidences — called spiritual fruit — of a Christ-follower.

In what ways do your thoughts, habits, and actions demonstrate that God's Word has been engrafted onto your heart?

What fruit of the Spirit are you currently producing?

Is any of the Spirit's fruit missing in your life?

Spending time with God will enable us to naturally develop and demonstrate the fruit of the Spirit. In this way, we won't have to strive to *get* the fruit of the Spirit — the fruit of the Spirit will *get* us.

Notes

True Christianity is a relationship with God through Jesus. And it's this relationship that allows our minds to be transformed and our behavior to be different so our secular culture won't leave its filthy marks on us. Rather, we'll interact with our culture by showing kindness and compassion, and we'll leave the love of Jesus on them.

Prayer

God, help me know

- what to do.
- what to say.
- what to think.
- where to go.

For Reflection

What did God reveal about His character?

How have you been challenged in a specific area of your life?

How will you apply the passage to your daily routine?

How is your faith being strengthened?

)(

It doesn't make sense to think we can remain unmarked by secular habits, but the power of the Holy Spirit enables us to put off old habits and reflect the character of Christ.

)(

Godly Friends Chime In

CAROL says, "My father daily immersed himself in God's Word and as a result, was able to demonstrate the fruit of the Spirit. He had many hard experiences in his growing-up years. He could have easily been a resentful, angry, man but he chose God's way. His quiet but firm demeanor, words of wisdom, and great reliance on God were a lasting example of what I wanted in my life.

"Years later, I got what I wanted. I convinced my husband, who had retired from teaching ahead of me, to substitute two days for me. After arriving home, he started to tell me about the day. But instead of telling me about my students, he told me about Tracey, the third-grade teacher who had stopped by to see me. 'She was surprised to see me,' he said, 'but stayed long enough to tell me that you had been a great help to her. Watching you and talking with you had encouraged her to seek the Lord.' That was my first realization that demonstrating the fruit of the Spirit, like my father did, had a significant impact on others who were watching."

- Trials are part of the Christian life.
- True religion is service and devotion to God.
- A humble servant is truly free.
- Joy comes from experiencing God's faithfulness.
- God provides wisdom to those who ask.
- God provides wisdom for every area of our life.
- A double-minded person's loyalty flips back and forth between God and the world.
- We can endure and persevere through the power of the Holy Spirit.
- Confess wicked thoughts before they give birth to sin and the subsequent consequences.
- Money has the potential to be more important than God.
- Our words speak emotional life or death.
- Inappropriate anger damages relationships.
- Sinful habits prevent us from enjoying new life in Christ.
- The condition of our hearts defines our relationship with God.
- Encourage, care, and serve others.
- We live in this world but should not be marked by it.
- The Holy Spirit enables us to resist conforming to expected cultural standards.
- We can and should humbly run to God.
- Take seriously God's command to love.
- We demonstrate God's love through a consistent lifestyle.
- We should love the engrafted Word.
- God transforms us from the inside.
- The fruit of the Spirit is evidence of a changed life.
- James desires to encourage and teach Christ-followers how to live out their faith.
- Hearing God's words and doing them is a sign of spiritual maturity.
- Put off old sinful behaviors and put on new Christ-like behaviors.
- God is good.
- God's purpose in testing is to transform us into the image of Christ.

16 Survival Tips for Trials

We all go through difficult times of suffering. Often, we call these times "storms." Maybe yours is a hurricane-type storm with lasting consequences, changing the landscape of your circumstances. Or perhaps your storm can be compared to a heavy rainstorm that keeps you inside all day.

First, when Jesus was in the boat with His disciples as a storm raged, Jesus stayed with them. And He stays with you, too (Mark 4:35–41).

Second, Jesus asked Peter to walk to Him. As long as Peter's focus was on Jesus, he walked. But the moment he looked away and saw the vastness of the sea, (the situation) he became afraid and began to sink. Keep your eyes on Jesus (Matthew 14:29).

All storms end eventually. But while you're waiting for the rainbow, here are 16 ways to help you get through your storm.

1. Make these two words your daily prayer: Help me. Praying these words admits humility and keeps your eyes turned to the heavenly Father.
2. Ask God to open your eyes to see what He wants you to see in your current situation. (Psalm 119:18).
3. Read a psalm. Many psalms boast of God's power and remind us of reasons to be joyful. Others are laments of sorrow, pain, sadness, and they help us feel less alone.
4. Place a sticky note on your mirror, the front door, the refrigerator, the dashboard in your car . . . any place you look regularly to remind you to trust in Him. Write things like:
   - God is working in my life and situation today.
   - *Be strong and do not give up, for your work will be rewarded* (2 Chronicles15:7).
   - God is enough.
   - *Some trust in chariots, and some in horses, but we trust in God* (Psalm 20:7–8). Today we could say, "Some trust in their attorney, their finances, or friends. But I trust the One with all the power."
   - God's strength is perfect in my weakness (2 Corinthians 12:9).
   - God is near me (Psalm 34:18).

5. Tell God the truth about how you are feeling, even if you're angry and disappointed. Then stand on God's truth that says:
    *   God loves you.
    *   God forgives you.
    *   God cares about you, your future, and the people you love.
    *   God is compassionate and will bring all things to their proper outcome.
6. Believe that God is powerful enough to carry you through your difficult circumstances and help you to find peace.
7. Spend extra time in prayer and Bible reading. *Unless God's Word had been my delight, I would have perished in my affliction* (Psalm 119:92–93).
8. Take it one day at a time.
9. Every time you are reminded of the magnitude of your problem say "Jesus" aloud.
10. Seek counseling from a professional counselor who seeks wisdom from God and will commit to pray for you.
11. Speak positively about your future aloud. *Though You have made me see troubles, many and bitter, you will restore my life again; from the depths of the earth you will again bring me up* (Psalm 71:20).
12. Guard your heart and mind by meditating on Scripture.
13. Confide in a friend who loves God and loves you. Choose someone who won't be intimidated to speak the truth or be worried about disagreeing, and who will hold you accountable.
14. Confess your sin. Then do not revisit your sins, grieving over them like tombstones in a cemetery.
15. Sing praise songs.
16. Make a list of things you are thankful for.

Week 2, Day 1

Love: It's Royal!

Read James 2:1–9:

> *My brethren, do not hold your faith in our glorious Lord Jesus Christ with an attitude of personal favoritism. For if a man comes into your assembly with a gold ring and dressed in fine clothes, and there also comes in a poor man in dirty clothes, and you pay special attention to the one who is wearing the fine clothes, and say, "You sit here in a good place," and you say to the poor man, "You stand over there, or sit down by my footstool," have you not made distinctions among yourselves, and become judges with evil motives? Listen, my beloved brethren: did not God choose the poor of this world to be rich in faith and heirs of the kingdom which He promised to those who love Him? But you have dishonored the poor man. Is it not the rich who oppress you and personally drag you into court? Do they not blaspheme the fair name by which you have been called? If, however, you are fulfilling the royal law according to the Scripture, "YOU SHALL LOVE YOUR NEIGHBOR AS YOURSELF," you are doing well. But if you show partiality, you are committing sin and are convicted by the law as transgressors.*

*M*y brethren. A sentiment used by James to address his fellow Christians. The way he "talks with" this group who placed their faith in Jesus is admirable. He shows them the tender side of being mutually supportive in their journey toward spiritual maturity. Similarly, we're sisters in Christ — a group of women who treasure the faith and follow Jesus' teachings. We choose to shine together.

What's cool is that many of us do online Bible study with women from other parts of the state, country, or world, and we're unfamiliar with any person's social class, education, external appearance, or even reputation. What we see and hear is the internal — or the heart. In this way we're truly impartial and avoid showing favoritism of any kind. Neither do we judge what we can't see. And that is the point James drives home: Don't be partial based on external appearances . . . especially the appearance of wealth.

Let's suppose, though, that we're participating in a face-to-face Bible study. An attractive woman wearing fashionable clothes with a vivacious, friendly personality enters your small group. She appears successful and happy.

Also visiting your group is a woman who seems stressed and weary. She adorns herself simply and appears to be unsure of her acceptance. Striving to be inconspicuous, she settles into the back chair in the corner of the room.

Which woman are you more drawn to and more likely to invite to lunch or to hang out?

If you were drawn to the disadvantaged woman who appeared to need help, why do you think you were drawn to her?

What about the successful-looking woman? If you were drawn to her, what were the reasons?

In fact, what are any reasons for selecting friends at a first encounter?

Besides the appearance of wealth and poverty, in what other ways do we judge one another?

Why do you think some women shun other women? What judgment do you think other women rush to make?

No matter which woman we chose to interact with in the example above, we may have shown favoritism. Favoritism is defined as "the unfair practice of treating some people better than others."[24] How can favoritism of one group or person lead to exclusion of another?

What reason(s) might a group of women have to exclude someone?

We may unintentionally exclude someone if we assume that person wouldn't choose us as a friend. That is also judgmental. When have you been wrongly judged?

First-century Christians were making judgments about one another based on external appearances only. They weren't drawing sound conclusions or judgments based on the Christ-like attributes a person demonstrated, such as the fruit of the Spirit that you recorded in James chapter one. We don't need to divert or backtrack, but it's important to look again at what is observable.

Revisit Galatians 5:22–23. Review the fruit of the Spirit.

As we've studied already in James chapter one, a person's wealth and success isn't always evidence of a worthy character. Poverty and failure don't always lead to a humble spirit either.

Christ-followers come from every aspect of society and every social class. The poorer aren't farther away from God, and the richer Christians aren't any closer. In addition, being rich doesn't make us good, and being poor doesn't make us bad.[25]

The message of this passage is for us to withhold judgment and, instead, love all people. In fact, the command to love is quoted nine times in the New Testament. James warns about choosing associates and friends in hopes of elevating our own or status. The law of love — also referred to as the Royal Law — is about respecting all people, regardless of wealth.

Wiersbe describes this kind of love. "Hatred makes a person a slave, but love sets us free from selfishness and enables us to reign like kings. Love enables us to obey the Word of God and to treat people as God commands us to do. We obey His Law, not out of fear, but out of love. Christian love does not mean that I must *like* a person and agree with him on everything. I may not like his vocabulary or his habits, and I may not want him as an intimate friend. Christian love means treating others the way God has treated me."[26]

God extends the hand of fellowship to all of us in His family. He isn't a partial God, who involves Himself in narrow or exclusive groups.

Notes

Prayer

God, help me know

- what to do.
- what to say.
- what to think.
- where to go.

For Reflection

What did God reveal about His character?

How have you been challenged in a specific area of your life?

How will you apply the passage to your daily routine?

How is your faith being strengthened?

Godly Friends Chime In

CAROL shares, "My fondest memory that applies to this passage is when my husband brought home an older woman, and her dog, whose car had broken down in the middle of an intersection in town. He and another man had pushed her car off to the side and then brought her to out house. He introduced her and said that she would be staying for dinner while he made arrangements for her car, and then he went to get Strompella, her dog, to introduce her to our dogs. I took one look at this woman and thought, Bag Lady. The woman set aside her big cloth bag and took off two sweaters. I hung up the clothing and asked my daughters to show her the bathroom, where she could tidy up for dinner. This lady ended up staying with us for a few days before her granddaughter was able to come and get her. My daughter and my boys played musical rooms so the lady could stay in her own room. In that short time, we heard her heart-wrenching story of coming with her first husband, now passed, to the United States from Germany, after the war. Only a short while before we met her, her second husband had been found dead, hidden under brush and leaves beside the road, a distance from his car. She was estranged from the second husband's children except for this granddaughter and her husband who still communicated with her. The Bag Lady turned out to be a lovely, lonely Christian lady. She became a friend and we had many good times when Grandma #3 came to visit. She was by no means a Bag Lady, but part of God's wonderful story."

JAN shares, "If it wasn't for God, I could judge people with the best of them — especially by their appearance or way of life. But God reminds me that Jesus loves us all, and I need to look at these people the way Jesus did — the way He looked at the woman at the well. I know in my heart that Jesus loves us all, but in my head I sometimes have trouble accepting it. When I first began to do prison visitations, it was incredibly difficult because my natural inclination was to judge. I had to turn back to God time and time again, knowing that to God my small sins are just as bad as the sin that got those people in prison. I constantly ask for forgiveness and God's help, and He is changing me from being the judgmental person I used to be."

Notes   CINDY says, "The topic of judging others is convicting, but I feel it especially when I hear more about the situation or what that person has gone through. But I'm also a people pleaser, so at the same time I have a fear of being judged. I sometimes find I will keep silent as a result of my fear. I strive to be mindful and listen to the Holy Spirit and speak when prompted."

Week 2, Day 2

Sin: Major, Minor, Everything in Between

Read James 2:10–13:

> *Whoever keeps the whole law and yet stumbles in one point, he has become guilty of all. For He who said, "Do not commit adultery," also said, "Do not commit murder." Now if you do not commit adultery, but do commit murder, you have become a transgressor of the law. So speak and so act as those who are to be judged by the law of liberty. For judgment will be merciless to one who has shown no mercy; mercy triumphs over judgment.*

In 2012 *The Atlantic* conducted a survey to gauge where Americans stood on what they considered to be the worst sin. A whopping 89 percent said that adultery wins the title.[27] Some may agree, others disagree, and a smattering don't want to discuss adultery at all. If you're in the latter group who doesn't want to talk about adultery, you'll be relieved to know, we aren't.

Today's passage discusses *sin* in general — what we might describe as the dangerous, serious, mediocre, and everything-in-between kind of sin. But our assessments of sin don't always align with God's view of sin. The Bible uses the Hebrew word *chata* for sin; it means "to miss the mark."[28] Not a little . . . or a lot . . . but to miss the mark in general. *Any and all sin* offends God and makes us sinful. We're imperfect people. My friend put it this way: You take a test and only miss one question; it's still not a perfect score.

Romans 3:23 tells us *all have sinned and fall short of the glory of God.*

I wouldn't blame you if you decided to skip this lesson. Sin — what it is or isn't along with its ramifications or consequences —

is a difficult topic. Often, discussion about sin leads to debate. Maybe you've said to yourself or heard others say, "I'm not so bad . . . I don't sin like her."

Being a sinner is the bad news — and we'll tackle the bad news first. But be encouraged because good news is right around the corner . . . or on the next few pages.

A person commits a sin when he or she deliberately chooses to practice a sinful lifestyle or make sin a habit.[29] All sin is toxic, and while James writes to Christ-followers who are saved and going to heaven, sin does affect the relationship we have with our heavenly Father. So, we needn't compare sins — God sees sin as a whole, and none of us is perfect. The person who doesn't commit murder or adultery shouldn't be self-righteous or think she is superior to anyone.

There is another side of sin — the sin of omission — when we don't do things we should . . . like failure to love others, for example.

All sin is offensive to God and has a price tag. The consequences for the Christ-follower who engages in habitual sin, however, can vary. How so?

For example, a gossiper's consequences can include loss of friendships; for the alcoholic, loss of income; for the adulterer, loss of family; for the addict, loss of purpose. Sin is destructive and although the consequences will vary, sin will always enslave us to someone or something.

Now that we've determined what sin is (missing the mark) and how we're guilty (none is perfect), you may wonder, *How, then, will we ever be free?* Now the good news: The law of liberty makes us free.

Wiersbe wrote, "Liberty does not mean license. License (doing whatever we want to do) is the worst kind of bondage. Liberty means freedom to be all that I can be in Jesus Christ. License is confinement; liberty is fulfillment."[30]

Liberty doesn't get rid of the Ten Commandments; it expands them to fulfill the greater law, which is to love God and others.

Read Matthew 22:37–39. And He said to him, *"YOU SHALL LOVE THE LORD YOUR GOD WITH ALL YOUR HEART, WITH ALL YOUR SOUL, AND WITH ALL YOUR MIND." This is the first and great commandment. And the second is like it: "YOU SHALL LOVE YOUR NEIGHBOR AS YOURSELF."*

Circle both commands.

The greatest law — the royal law — is to _____

_____.

By fulfilling the royal law, we've also fulfilled the obligation of all other laws. We wouldn't need the Ten Commandments if we kept the royal law — our love for God and others would compel us to naturally strive to keep the royal law and make living by it a life principle.

Therefore, the law of liberty frees us to live like Jesus. We obey God's Word by faith, not by self-effort or willpower, but by the power of the Holy Spirit. We're not enslaved to the law; we're free to live out our faith which proves our salvation.

How do you use your freedom to show your love for God?

While committing adultery is a serious sin, so is the sin of not loving others. Whatever sin has us captive — slander against another person or selfish ambition while climbing the corporate ladder — we need to repent of the sin that prevents us from freely living for Christ.

Read the words of King David: *When I kept silent about my sin, my body wasted away through my groaning all day long. For day and night Your hand was heavy upon me; my vitality was drained away as with the fever heat of summer. I acknowledged my sin to You, and my iniquity I did not hide; I said, "I will confess my transgressions to the Lord;" and You forgave the guilt of my sin* (Psalm 32:3–4).

Circle what happened to David's body as a result of sin. Whose hand was pressing on him?

What did King David finally do that restored his relationship with God?

How did God respond?

Sin eclipses our sweet fellowship with God. Read Psalm 66:18 and fill in the missing words:

If I regard _____ in my heart, The Lord will not _____ .

Depending on the Bible translation you're using, you may have read, *wickedness* (NASB), *iniquity* (KJV), *malice* (CSB), or *sin* (NIV).

How does sin break fellowship with God?

But because of God's great love for us, we can seek God's forgiveness and receive His mercy. We can pray:

Psalm 51:2 — *Wash me thoroughly from my iniquity and cleanse me from my sin.*

Psalm 51:7–12 — *Cleanse me with hyssop, and I will be clean; wash me, and I will be whiter than snow. Let me hear joy and gladness; let the bones you have crushed rejoice. Hide your face from my sins and blot out all my iniquity. Create in me a pure heart, O God, and renew a steadfast spirit within me. Do not cast me from your presence or take your Holy Spirit from me. Restore to me the joy of your salvation and grant me a willing spirit, to sustain me.* (NIV)

Ezekiel 36:25 — *I will sprinkle clean water on you, and you will be clean; I will cleanse you from all your filthiness and from all your idols.*

The Hebrew word for purify is *barar*, which means "to cleanse; purge."[31] Is there a sinful attitude, habit, disposition, or action in your life that needs to be removed?

Digging deep into the heart and searching for sin, either recognizable or obscure, might not be easy, but it's a necessary step to confession. Why do you think some people choose to live independent from God rather than confront their sin?

Read Micah 7:18 and fill in the missing words:

Who is a God like you, who _____ of the remnant of his inheritance? You do not stay _____ forever but delight to show _____ (NIV).

When we confess and repent of sin, God shows mercy and an intimate relationship with God is restored. And because God shows mercy to us, we can show mercy to others.

Notes

✕

It doesn't make sense that forgiveness of sin is as simple as asking for it, but God's mercy and love make forgiveness of sin possible.

✕

Prayer

God, help me know

- what to do.
- what to say.
- what to think.
- where to go.

For Reflection

What did God reveal about His character?

How have you been challenged in a specific area of your life?

How will you apply the passage to your daily routine?

How is your faith being strengthened?

Godly Friends Chime In

MEG speaks up. "It's so easy for me to focus on the sins that are being committed that I sometimes forget about the sin of omission — the things I don't do. I've been very convicted! I blamed my apathy on negative personality traits I was born with. I hadn't thought about how some of those traits can be sinful."

SAVANNAH says, "I am strongly convicted that all sin is missing the mark and offensive to God. But I'm also overjoyed that God helps me become aware of my sin so I can confess it and I can be in a right relationship with God. I am so glad that He helps me!"

Week 2, Day 3

Compelled to Obey

Read James 2:14–20

What use is it, my brethren, if someone says he has faith but he has no works? Can that faith save him? If a brother or sister is without clothing and in need of daily food, and one of you says to them, "Go in peace, be warmed and be filled," and yet you do not give them what is necessary for their body, what use is that? Even so faith, if it has no works, is dead, being by itself. But someone may well say, "You have faith and I have works; show me your faith without the works, and I will show you my faith by my works." You believe that God is one. You do well; the demons also believe, and shudder. But are you willing to recognize, you foolish fellow, that faith without works is useless?

When I returned home from work, a flurry of people and several cars crowded my driveway.

"Your dad's been in an accident," Alan said. The look in his eyes and his silence spoke volumes. He began to cry and then I knew that my father was dead. I moaned loudly while my husband held me.

"How?" I managed to ask. "Robbery attempt. He was shot through the heart and killed instantly." I felt emotions I'd never felt. I hated the men who murdered my father. Darkness descended around me.

After my father's funeral, life fell back into its normal routines — except there was nothing normal about what I was feeling. I suppressed my hate and continued my morning routine — an early 5:30 A.M. devotion and prayer time with God.

One morning the words of John 14:15 jumped off the page: *"If you love Me, you will keep My commandments."* With genuine affection I responded, I love You, God! Even as I said it, I stammered. The emotion surprised me so much that I looked around the room to see if God was looking. Weird, right?

Yet something was wrong, and I knew what it was. First John 4:7 tells us to love one another. I was being disobedient. Tears spilled from my eyes and left wet splotches on my open Bible.

> *I don't hate anyone — I strongly dislike them!* I protested. I continued my justifying rant. *They deserve to be hated for the crimes they have committed.*
>
> But in the stillness and quiet of the morning, God changed my heart. My love for God moved me to sorrow. I admitted what I had been hiding and began to understand that loving God meant obeying Him. Obedience required love —for the men who had murdered my father.

*I*ntentionally or not, we all sin. Romans 3:10 tells us: *There is no one righteous, not even one* (NIV). And recall Romans 3:23: *For all have sinned and fall short of the glory of God.*

From the moment sin entered the world, however, God made provision for us to be free from the bondage of sin. He gave His son, Jesus, to pay the debt for our sin. When we place faith in God and accept that Jesus died on the cross for our sin, we become Christians — Christ followers. We cannot work for salvation; it's a gift.

Reflect on today's passage, then fill in the blank.

_____ saved me — not my good

_____.

In Ephesians 2:8–9 Paul wrote: *By grace you have been saved through faith; and that not of yourselves, it is the gift of God; not as a result of works, so that no one may boast.*

Paul was referring to the law of Moses — we're no longer under law; we are saved by grace. James explains we're not judged for our sin, but fellowship with God is broken until we confess our sin.

Since God's grace already saved us, why should we do good works and obey His commands? In Romans 6:1 Paul asked this rhetorical question: *What shall we say then? Are we to continue in sin so that grace may increase?* How would you respond to Paul's question?

Reread James 2:17. If our faith doesn't produce good works, then our faith is _____.

What do you think that means?

Romans 4:4 tells us that our work isn't for salvation, but an obligation compelled by love. What motivates you to do good works?

As a loving Father, God established boundaries for His children to live within. God's boundaries provide security. God knows that physically, spiritually, emotionally, and mentally, we'll live better when we obey them. When we choose to ignore the boundaries, however, God chastens the disobedient. When we choose to obey, He blesses. But either way, He is manifesting His love.

Author and pastor John Piper says, "Our obedience is God's pleasure when it proves that God is our treasure. This is good news, because it means very simply that the command to obey is the command to be happy in God. The commandments of God are only as hard to obey as the promises of God are hard to believe. The Word of God is only as hard to obey as the beauty of God is hard to cherish."[32]

Are you happy in God? How do you explain this?

Believing there is a God isn't enough motivation for us to live out our faith. After all, the demons believe in God but they don't do any good works (James 2:19). Believing that Jesus' willingness to go to the cross was the ultimate act of obedience that paid our sin debt and that compels us to love Him back. We return His love by doing what He says is right.

Sometimes, though, it's not what we do that displeases God but what we don't do. By rejecting God's command to love others, I was living in disobedience. But because I loved God more than I hated the men that murdered my father, I prayed and asked God how to get rid of my hate and obey Him. God drew me to Ephesians 6:12. I learned that Satan was the real enemy, and I could transfer my hate to him. My hate for the people who took my father from me began to dissipate and, over time, vanished altogether.

When do you feel obedience is too hard?

When God tells us to behave in a specific way or adopt a certain attitude, He also empowers us to do it. The Holy Spirit provides the strength. With confidence, we can be obedient and please God with our responses. Thankfully, we're not responsible for other people's behaviors. We do what God says to do, then leave the consequences to Him.

As we grow in our relationship with Him, He shows us specific, unique ways to obey Him. For example, our love for God might compel us to:

- step out of our comfort zone and serve.
- practice self-control.
- withdraw from gossip.
- begin a new habit or stop one.
- surrender our desires and seek His desires.
- forgive or put aside hate.
- resist shyness and boldly share our faith.
- pray for our enemy.
- teach a class.
- write a book or foster a child.
- start a prayer group.

What is God calling you to do?

Our obedience requires a close relationship with God so we can hear His voice.

How would you describe your relationship with God? Check all that apply.

- ❑ Distant
- ❑ Occasional conversation
- ❑ He's let me down
- ❑ Weekly church attendance or Bible study
- ❑ Daily conversation and Bible reading
- ❑ I don't always understand, but I'm learning to trust
- ❑ I'm dependent on His leading every day

Obeying God isn't difficult when we agree with His plan or it suits our purpose. And it's easy to avoid doing what we think is wrong or doesn't appeal to us. When has obedience been costly, illogical, or inconvenient for you?

Describe how you can you show your faith through works while at work, home, and church.

How can you show your faith when you're hanging out with non-Christian friends?

How would you describe a person who talks about loving God but doesn't obey His commands?

We're promised blessings when we choose to live by God's commands. Read the passages about the reward for obedience and complete the "*if . . . then*" promise:

Passage	If	Then
Deuteronomy 4:5–6		
Deuteronomy 6:25		
Deuteronomy 28:1–2		
Deuteronomy 28:1–2		
Deuteronomy 30:9–11		
Joshua 1:7		
Isaiah 1:19		
Isaiah 48:18		
Jeremiah 7:23		

God loves all of His children equally. There are additional blessings, however, for those who obey His commands. We'll never lose His love, but we could forfeit a blessing.

So much of the book of Joshua reads like an optimistic pep talk. In fact, four times in Joshua chapter one, we're told to be "strong and courageous." Joshua 1:8 specifically defines success: *This book of the law shall not depart from your mouth, but you shall meditate on it day and night, so that you may be careful to do according to all that is written in it; for then you will make your way prosperous, and then you will have success.*

Interestingly, in Hebrew, success means wisdom.[33] According to this verse, what makes a person successful (wise)?

Is this your current habit? If not, what will you do to put this into practice? If so, when, where, and how do you read, mediate, reflect on, and memorize Scripture?

Loving God means we commit to spend time with Him and strive to do what He says. Then we'll enjoy the blessings that accompany obedience.

Prayer

God, help me know

- what to do.
- what to say.
- what to think.
- where to go.

For Reflection

What did God reveal about His character?

How have you been challenged in a specific area of your life?

How will you apply the passage to your daily routine?

How is your faith being strengthened?

)(

It doesn't always make sense to step out of our comfort zone and do what God says to do, but our love for Him compels us to obey and when we do, we shine more brightly.

)(

Godly Friends Chime In:

SAVANNAH opens up, "I see clearly in my own life when I truly began to obey God. Before this, I was going through the motions of going to church, and then living back in the world. So my relationship with God was limited to an hour and half of church. It was distant. Being "saved by grace and not by works" made me feel like I still could do whatever I wanted. It was a stumbling block for me, because I misunderstood. I was really wrong! I can believe in God all I want, but if my lifestyle isn't showing evidence that Jesus lives in me, then I must be spiritually dead. Apart from God, I am nothing! Faith with works shows in our lifestyle — in our conversations, conduct, and character. Obedience came easier for me when I just wanted to please the Father. Not only that, but the Holy Spirit has a way of making me feel "off" when I've spoken inappropriately or acted in a messy way. His corrections come so clear. Obedience truly makes us happy. When I began a genuine walk with the Lord, I was able to obey. And when I sin, I am also able to come to the Lord for forgiveness. What a good, good Father we have!"

MEG agrees. "I'm reminded of 1 Thessalonians 5:24: *"The One who calls you is faithful, and He will do it."* I was challenged to look at the people who have hurt me and realize that God loves them just as much as He loves me and that I needed to love them too."

Week 2, Day 4

A Friend of God

Read James 2:21–24

Was not Abraham our father justified by works when he offered up Isaac his son on the altar? You see that faith was working with his works, and as a result of the works, faith was perfected; and the Scripture was fulfilled which says, "ABRAHAM BELIEVED GOD, AND IT WAS RECKONED TO HIM AS RIGHTEOUSNESS," and he was called the friend of God. You see that a man is justified by works and not by faith alone.

*H*ave you ever thought about what you'd like to have inscribed on your headstone? Imagine the honor of having this epitaph: *She was a friend of God.* Webster's defines friend as "a favored companion."[34] This was Abraham's legacy. What do you think is required to be known as God's friend?

Let's examine the habits of Abraham, the owner of this prestigious title.

Read Genesis 22:1–14, the passage depicting Abraham's offering of Isaac. Match the verses to Abraham's behavior.

_____	Genesis 22:	A. He obeyed
_____	Genesis 22:3	B. He listened
_____	Genesis 22:5	C. He worshipped
_____	Genesis 22:12	D. He believed God would provide
_____	Genesis 22:14	E. He feared

Why do you think James revisited Abraham's journey to offer up Isaac on the altar?

What can you conclude about Abraham's mindset?

Read Genesis 18:22–33. Who formulated the negotiations and asked all the questions?

What does Abraham's bold approach reveal about his safety and security in God?

Read Hebrews 6:12–15. What virtue is ascribed to Abraham?

Go over a few chapters and read Hebrews 11:8–17. Abraham is credited with _____
that is evidenced by his_____
_____.

Based on these passages, what can you conclude about Abraham's character?

The *Women's Evangelical Commentary* says, "James stressed the deeds during Abraham's lifespan as evidence of his complete trust in God. Genuine faith will produce works, and works complete faith. Abraham demonstrated his faith by his work of obedience. James used the word *justified* in the sense of proving — you prove or testify to others of your genuine faith through acts of obedience."[35]

Awesome. Obedience proves how much we trust God. When obedience is motivated by trust, our good works are justified.

Matthew Henry wrote, "A justifying faith cannot be without works, and Abraham is one of two examples [in this chapter]. By what Abraham did, it appeared that he truly believed. The faith of Abraham was a working faith. You see then how that by works a man is justified, and not by faith only; not by believing without obeying, but by having such a faith as is productive of good works . . . the actions of faith make it grow perfect as the truth of faith makes it act. Such an acting faith will make others, as well as Abraham, friends of God."[36]

We previously defined friend as a "favored companion." As we spend time with our favored friend, we develop a special bond and our trust in that friend grows stronger. Abraham became spiritually mature because he spent time with the Lord — and created the bond of friendship. And although Abraham's son was spared, both Abraham and God manifested love that's required to sacrifice a beloved son — the love of God for His people, and a person's love of God.

What steps, if any, are you taking to achieve spiritual maturity?

God's Word gives us hope! Read Romans 4:18–22: *In hope against hope he believed, so that he might become a father of many nations according to that which had been spoken, "So shall your descendants be." Without becoming weak in faith he contemplated his own body, now as good as dead since he was about a hundred years old, and the deadness of Sarah's womb; yet, with respect to the promise of God, he did not waver in unbelief but grew strong in faith, giving glory to God, and being fully assured that what God had promised, He was able also to perform. Therefore it was also credited to him as righteousness.*

How would you describe Abraham's response to God's prophecy? How does this passage bring you hope?

Abraham was a friend of God, and we can be His friend, too, when we:

- Patiently wait. *Wait for the LORD; be strong and let your heart take courage; yes, wait for the LORD.* Psalm 27:14

- Listen for His voice. *Oh that My people would listen to Me, that Israel would walk in My ways!* Psalm 81:13

- Worship Him. *Come, let us worship and bow down, let us kneel before the LORD OUR MAKER.* Psalm 95:6

- Call on Him. *And it will come about that whoever calls on the name of the Lord will be delivered.* Joel 2:32

- Trust Him to provide. *And my God will supply all your needs according to His riches in glory in Christ Jesus.* Philippians 4:19

- Obey His commands. *You are My friends if you do what I command you. No longer do I call you slaves, for the slave does not know what his master is doing; but I have called you friends, for all things that I have heard from My Father I have made known to you.* John 15:14–15

- Reverence Him. *To man He said, 'Behold, the fear of the Lord, that is wisdom.* Job 28:28

- Have faith. *So that your faith would not rest on the wisdom of men, but on the power of God.* 1 Corinthians 2:5

- Believe. *These have been written so that you may believe that Jesus is the Christ, the Son of God; and that believing you may have life in His name.* John 20:31

Each acts as a symptom of working faith. And working faith makes us friends of God.

Prayer

God, help me know

- what to do.
- what to say.
- what to think.
- where to go.

For Reflection

What did God reveal about His character?

How have you been challenged in a specific area of your life?

How will you apply the passage to your daily routine?

How is your faith being strengthened?

⋊

It doesn't make sense that we can enjoy the bond of friendship with Almighty God, but faith in God makes friendship possible.

⋊

Godly Friends Chime In

SAVANNAH says, "I want 'She was a favored companion of God' on my headstone! Actions and faith make me righteous. I am able to see why I stumbled so much a few years ago. I didn't spend but an hour each week with God. I had no wisdom, and no fear of the Lord either. I never obeyed His commands and I continued to live the way I wanted. I never grew spiritually. I praise God for His longsuffering that I was able to wake up and repent and start putting Him first. Thank You, Father. I want to have faith like Abraham."

CHARLA says, "This makes me think deeply about friendship in general and how I measure up in my daily life — how much trust, faith, patience, and listening skills do I demonstrate to my friends? It also reminds me that each friendship in our lives is precious and to be honored, with none being more precious than that friendship we have with God. What would our world be like if we all aspired to be, 'a friend of God'? Absolutely amazing!"

Week 2, Day 5

Leave It All Behind

Read James 2:25–26:

> *In the same way, was not Rahab the harlot also justified by works when she received the messengers and sent them out by another way? For just as the body without the spirit is dead, so also faith without works is dead.*

*E*ach of us leaves a legacy — being remembered or known for something. Abraham is remembered for his faith; Rahab is remembered for her sin. Yet…

From the start, Rahab is identified as a harlot, or a promiscuous woman. She lived in Jericho, the gateway city to Canaan. Her home, nestled within the thick walls that surrounded Jericho, was used as a place to entertain men. While engaged with the locals and tourists alike, Rahab heard things. One story that impacted her was the one told about how the God of the Israelite had dried up the Red Sea so they could escape from their Egyptian slave masters.

God prepared Rahab's heart long before she decided to serve Him. The tidbits of gossip that circulated throughout the town where she lived turned out to be true nuggets of wisdom, which Rahab embraced within her heart.

Let's meet her. Read Joshua 2:1–21. Joshua, the appointed leader of the Israelites, sent two spies into Jericho to check out the city. By God's divine intervention, they found safety in Rahab's house.

Where did Rahab hide the spies? (v. 6)

Why did she decide to rescue them? (vv. 8–10)

In whom did she trust? (v. 11)

What did she ask in exchange for hiding them? (vv. 12–13)

How did the spies respond to her request? (v. 14)

What did Rahab use to enable the spies to escape? (v. 15)

What warning did she give them? (v. 16)

The men said they would honor Rahab's request if she put what in the window upon their return? (v. 18)

What evidence was there to prove she would honor their request and their God? (v. 21)

Why do you think the spies trusted Rahab enough to promise to return and save her?

Notes

Rahab's actions, words, warnings, and responses, give us insight into her character. Circle the words that describe Rahab:

Clever	Lazy	Faithful	Receptive
Energetic	Wise	Reckless	Sick
Believer	Eager	Passionate	Arrogant
Interested	Trusting	Risk-taker	Courageous

Other_____

And think about her residence — a remodel that transformed her home from a place of scandalous behavior to a lighthouse on a hill.

On the seventh day, Israel was ready for battle. Rahab heard the sound from the rams' horns, and the city walls shattering. Can you imagine the mayhem outside of Rahab's window? What do you think was going through Rahab's mind?

Fast forward to Joshua chapter six. The city had been destroyed; its people were defeated. When the battle was over, what happened to Rahab and her family? (vv. 22–25)

Rahab left everything behind, lived for God, and became an ancestor in the line of Jesus (Matthew 1:5). What saved Rahab? Her faith? Her actions? Both? Explain your thinking.

In what ways did Rahab engage in reckless behavior?

How are we sometimes like Rahab?

The evidence of Rahab's faith in God was in a single red rope. How do we know that she changed directions and went a new way? She convinced her family to believe in the God of Abraham and her entire household was rescued. Her first mission experience was to her family.

We're all missionaries — shining the light on the wondrous things God has done. And now, we're even more like Rahab — examples and prayer warriors for our family — immediate, extended, and adopted. How does that encourage you?

How are you motivated to share wisdom and the truth of God with your family?

Read Hebrews 11:30–31. In this passage, whose name is the only name recorded from Jericho?

What was Rabab's new legacy?

Out of the whole city, God spared a prostitute and her family. What does that say about God?

What does Rahab's life story show us? Can we go another way?

Both Rahab and the spies took risks. When we choose to go a different direction, we also take risks. How might doing things differently be a risk for you?

What, if anything, is holding you back from fully submitting to God?

God doesn't wait until we are mature in faith or until we're perfect (that's not happening in this world) before He uses us. He used Rahab to complete His purpose and He will use us too if we're willing to go a different direction, take a risk in the area of the unknown, and triumph over fear to answer God's call.

Are you ready to accept nuggets of truth and power over widespread lies? If yes, how will you allow God to use you, especially when going a new direction means to leaving the past behind?

Perhaps you could tie a red ribbon around something (like a flower pot) to remind you to keep the faith. Rahab proved her faith by sending the spies another way and abandoning the habits of her former life. As a result, she is recorded in history not that of a harlot — but as a woman of faith.

Prayer

God, help me know

- what to do.
- what to say.
- what to think.
- where to go.

For Reflection

What did God reveal about His character?

How have you been challenged in a specific area of your life?

How will you apply the passage to your daily routine?

How is your faith being strengthened?

ж

*Often it doesn't
make sense to
withdraw from our
current situation
or abandon our
bad habits and go
another way, but
if we allow God
to plant His truth
within our hearts,
He will empower
us to respond as
women of faith and
become a light that
points others to
God.*

ж

Godly Friends Chime In

SAVANNAH says, "I'm getting my red ribbon! I see myself in Rahab. Her reputation was messy, but her faith compelled her to take bold actions. God hand-walked Rahab and her entire family out of the city untouched because she had believed wholeheartedly. This gives me goosebumps. She shifted — took risks by putting her life on the line because she believed. Again, faith plus action is life. God is a loving Father who keeps His promises. He watches those who believe, have faith in Him, and obey His way. Mayhem could be right outside our windows. There could be chaos and storms, but He has us covered. We can always turn directions, go another way, make the change. No matter how reckless we've been, God is long-suffering. He never gives up! It's so comforting to know that God doesn't wait for our full maturity in faith before uses us."

MEG shares, "There was a season in my life when I was angry with God. I'd been praying for weeks for my Grammy's health to improve and for God to heal her. But she died anyway, and my faith shattered into a million pieces. How was my Grammy dying a good thing? Didn't God care? Didn't He hear my prayers? I grew angry with God and hesitant to trust Him. I questioned my faith. As the months drew on, I drifted away from God. Then one day I realized I had no one else to turn to. Cautiously, I looked to God and He was there, with great understanding, patiently waiting for me to return. I left my questions behind and started a new, trusting relationship with God."

Truths from James 2

- Refrain from favoritism, judgment, and partiality based on external appearances.
- We base facts on evidences.
- Evidence of our faith is visible to other people.
- God's law is love.
- All sin offends God.
- Sin carries consequences.
- Obedience brings blessings.
- God pardons sins when we confess them.
- God mercy toward us compels us to show mercy to others.
- We are saved by faith in Jesus.
- Genuine faith compels us to do good works.
- Our faith means we must put love for others into action.
- God has a plan and purpose for each life.
- Abraham obeyed God.
- God called Abraham His friend.
- Rahab was compelled to do good works.
- Seek God about everything.
- We're saved by grace and pleased to obey.
- Each day is a new beginning.
- The law of liberty frees us to live for Christ.
- The royal law is to love others.
- God prepares our hearts for useful service.

Years ago, my beloved pastor, Dr. Billy H. Cline, gave me a list of sins, explaining that often we don't check our hearts for less obvious sins. I never knew if he wrote this list himself or if another person gave the list to him. I've adapted his original list for our use.

Sin: An Attitude of the Heart

All a man's ways seem right to him but the Lord weighs the heart. Proverbs 21:2

Are we hiding any of these sins?

unbelief	fear	pride	jealousy
selfishness	worry	conceit	self-centeredness
hypocrisy	insecurity	ingratitude	self-justification
dishonesty	defensiveness	laziness	self-righteousness
controlling nature	demanding	unloving	selfish ambition
fear of people	busyness	insensitivity	self-protection
being judgmental	arrogance	rebelliousness	self-reliance
anger	strong will	rationalization	self-deception
unrepentance	apathy	anxiety	self-absorption
perfectionism	fake	withdrawal	self-sufficiency
despair	defeatism	a temper	self-pity
overbearing nature	unreliableness	deceitfulness	self-indulgence
inattentiveness	manipulation	doubt	irritability
envy	condemning nature	greed	condescending
unaccepting	poor listening	procrastination	irresponsibility
ignoring	breaking promises	being impolite	being disrespectful
resentfulness	love of preeminence	inconsistency	being uncaring
touchiness	making excuses	stubbornness	bondage to reputation
hatefulness	idolatry	a critical spirit	impatience
coldness	unrest	spitefulness	lust
overly sensitive	prejudice	favoritism	independence
excluding others	strife	domination	sulking/pouting
blame shifting	avoiding conflict	refusing to forgive	seeking approval
dogmatism	being abrasive	counting grievances	
undermining others	lacking compassion	lacking perseverance	
refusing to accept correction		disregard for others schedules	
insisting on own way		failure to recognize another's importance	

Out of the overflow of the heart the mouth speaks. Matthew 12:34

What about these sins of the mouth?

gossip	accusation	harshness	criticism
complaining	boasting	defending	arguing
mocking	slandering	lying	quarrelsomeness
bragging	swearing	insulting	unkind words
sarcasm	belittling	rudeness	nagging
provoking			

If you continue in my word, you are truly my disciples, and you will know the truth and the truth will make you free. John 8:31–32

God is light and in Him is no darkness at all. If we say we have fellowship with Him while we walk in darkness, we lie and do not live according to the truth; but if we walk in the light, as He is in the light, we have fellowship with one another, and the blood of Jesus His Son cleanses us from all sin. 1 John 1:5–7

Week 3, Day 1

A Woman of Influence

Read James 3:1:

Let not many of you become teachers, my brethren, knowing that as such we will incur a stricter judgment.

*T*he focus of this entire chapter is the destruction or edification that comes out of our mouths. But James begins with a warning to a group of people who use their words for a living: teachers and preachers. Both teachers and preachers influence others. Each position carries authority, and people listen to them.

You might think, *Oh good, I'm off the hook — I'm neither of these.* Not so fast. *The Matthew Henry Commentary* expands verse one to include the following: "Those who profess religion ought especially govern their tongues. True wisdom makes men meek . . . and herby it may easily be distinguished from a wisdom that is earthly."[37]

Do *you* profess religion? More specifically, do you confess to be a Christ-follower?

If you answered yes, take some extra time and think about how your words matter to all people, especially those who are unsure about what they believe. As we mature spiritually, God may provide more opportunities for us to share the gospel through our testimony and personal experiences. Sometimes we'll listen to others as a humble learner, and sometimes we'll speak up as a master teacher. And you may discover that when you interact with others, you're doing so not only as a friend but also as a mentor.

After the resurrection, Jesus appeared to the disciples and commissioned them. Read Mark 16:15. What did Jesus commission them to do?

As followers of Christ, we're to take seriously the opportunities we have to teach, preach, and share about how Jesus Christ has been, and is, the transforming power in our lives. We're all commissioned to tell our salvation story.

In Jesus' day, the scribes and Pharisees were influential leaders. They can be described this way:

Scribe   A person who wrote with the duty of multiplying copies of the law and of teaching it to others.

Pharisee A member of an educated group of priests or religious leaders distinguished by strict observance of the traditional and written law.

The scribes and Pharisees are often grouped together in the New Testament. The Pharisees wrongly expanded and interpreted the meaning of particular Mosaic laws. In the context of verse one, James talks about the dangerous effect that educated people, like the scribes and Pharisees can have on others. They misused language and spoke incorrectly, faked their actions so they looked better than they were, and misguided and wrongly influenced anyone who was watching or listening.

See for yourself. Read Matthew 23:1–34, then on the next page match the reference to the scribes and Pharisees sinful behavior.

_____ Matthew 23:1–3

A. You tell others what to do but you don't do it yourself.

_____ Matthew 23:4

B. You inflict heavy burdens on the people with so many rules, but you refuse to help them.

_____ Matthew 23:5–7

C. You strap leather boxes of Scripture to your arms and forehead to exalt yourself, gloat, and appear righteous.

_____ Matthew 23:13–14

D. You attend celebratory feasts and insist on the best seat.

_____ Matthew 23:15

E. You exempt yourself from God's law.

_____ Matthew 23:16–22

F. You lead others astray with false ideas.

_____ Matthew 23:23–24

G. You look for ways to break oaths.

_____ Matthew 23:25–28

H. You obsess over petty rules but neglect what is important: mercy, justice, and faith.

_____ Matthew 23:29–34

I. You cleanse the outside of your body to appear pure but your heart is filthy.

J. You murder God's prophets yet still feel worthy to sit in Moses' seat (a place of authority).

Matthew 23 tells us Jesus used strong language to discipline these educated teachers and leaders. He said, "Woe to you." *Woe* means "God's judgment." How many times does Jesus say *woe*?

Jesus condemned the scribes and Pharisees because they appeared to be righteous but their hearts were wicked.

Actions can lie; the heart cannot. We can fool people, but we can't fool God. 1 Samuel 16:7 tells us what the Lord said to Samuel: *Do not look at his appearance or at the height of his stature, because I have rejected him; for God sees not as man sees, for man looks at the outward appearance, but the LORD looks at the heart.*

How would you explain the meaning of this verse to a child?

Speaking of hypocrites, read Romans 2:21. In what way do you feel like a child being called to the teacher's desk to be disciplined?

This verse sounds similar to what we've previously read in James 1:22: *Prove yourselves doers of the word, and not merely hearers who delude themselves.* How does this verse convict or compel you to align your heart and mouth and truth?

Words matter. So does the heart's condition. What is your gut reaction to the word hypocrite?

In what ways can we sometimes behave like the Pharisees?

Why do you think people pretend to be something they're not?

How does social media enable people to hide truth and live a lie?

Do you ever pretend? If yes, when and where?

Do you think the church can be a place where people hide their true selves? Why or why not?

What, if anything, are you hiding?

First John 1:9 tells us *if we confess our sins, He is faithful and righteous to forgive us our sins and to cleanse us from all unrighteousness*. We don't have to run and hide in shame. We can run to Him for forgiveness.

Whether we're trained as a teacher, prepared as a preacher, or a willing person who shines the light of the gospel, we're all people of influence who can point others to Jesus Christ.

Prayer

God, help me know

- what to do.
- what to say.
- what to think.
- where to go.

Reflection

What did God reveal about His character?

How have you been challenged in a specific area of your life?

How will you apply the passage to your daily routine?

How is your faith being strengthened?

Ж

It doesn't make sense that God would empower us to influence other people, but because Christ lives in us, we can have a radiant impact on those within our sphere of influence.

Ж

Godly Friends Chime In

SAVANNAH says, "My study Bible notes says that the book of James exposes hypocritical practices. Each morning I've been searching my heart for any hypocritical behavior. I realized I had a lot of impurities lurking in my heart — some so hidden that I even kept them from myself. But I'm dealing with this sin now because the Holy Spirit has exposed them. I don't want to hold onto these any longer. I'm so thankful for the Holy Spirit's convictions."

CHARLA chimes in, "I remember singing "O be careful little eyes what you see . . . ." as a child. "O be careful little ears what you hear . . . tongue what you say . . . hands what you do . . . feet where you go . . . heart who you trust . . . mind what you think." As Christ-followers, we must be careful of all these, whether or not we are teachers or preachers. To some, we *are* the model of what a Christ-follower is — our actions, words, etc. all determine how well we model the behavior of someone who is following Christ. We may be the *only* model some people have!

Week 3, Day 2

Under Control

Read James 3:2–5

We all stumble in many ways. If anyone does not stumble in what he says, he is a perfect man, able to bridle the whole body as well. Now if we put the bits into the horses' mouths so that they will obey us, we direct their entire body as well. Look at the ships also, though they are so great and are driven by strong winds, are still directed by a very small rudder wherever the inclination of the pilot desires. So also the tongue is a small part of the body, and yet it boasts of great things. See how great a forest is set aflame by such a small fire!

I admit it.

At the onset of writing the James 3:2–5 lesson, I abruptly stopped and decided to clean the bathroom. And while I swished the brush around the inside of the toilet, it dawned on me that I actually chose to clean a toilet over confronting the sin and destruction that follow hurtful words. My deep conviction cheered my escape.

But we must not turn our backs on this truth, or hide in the bathroom to avoid acknowledging it. If we're going to move forward on our spiritual journey, we must boldly deal with this problem.

Maybe you've heard the adage "sticks and stones may break my bones, but words can never hurt me." Written originally as a children's rhyme in the early 1800's, it was meant to help those being bullied by insults.[38] A better adage might be what a shy first-grade girl wrote when she and her classmates were given parts of adages and asked to finish them: Sticks and stones may break your bones, but words can break your heart. In an age of bullying, we must take seriously how our words affect others.

Like me, you've probably watched children suffer with the pain of hurtful criticism and verbal insults. Perhaps you personally experienced the heartache of insensitive, careless words. Maybe you regret that you have used words haphazardly yourself.

Despite knowing the devastation hurtful words cause, people wield this weapon in nearly every social setting. We may use destructive words intentionally, or they may creep into the conversation in a subtle, unplanned way.

Why do you think James warned his friends about the destruction of the tongue?

We share another similarity with the first-century believers, but warnings about the tongue's power go back much further than first-century Christianity. Solomon wrote in Proverbs 12:18: ***There is one who speaks rashly like the thrusts of a sword, but the tongue of the wise brings healing.***

To what does he compare hurtful words?

Ouch! Words — spoken, typed, or texted — can trigger such devastation that the collateral damage results in emotional death. When have you been at the receiving end of verbal daggers? How did it make you feel?

Has there been a time someone's words, whether spoken accidentally, in a passive aggressive tone, or deliberately, discouraged you? Is so, what did you do, or not do?

How can tone of voice be equally damaging?

Now contrast those words with the uplifting, kind words someone spoke to you. What was said and how did you respond?

James compared the power our tongue possesses with two other powerful inanimate objects. Reread James 3:3. What do people who work with horses put in a horse's mouth, and what is the item's purpose?

The other object is revealed in James 3:4. What guides a ship?

A bit and rudder are small tools, yet they possess great power and determine the direction a horse or boat will go. How is the tongue like these small tools?

What else does James say is very small? (v. 5)

Maybe you've seen the news reports about the raging fires that swept through Australia beginning in September 2019. The fires resulted in the deaths of people and animals, widespread homelessness, and the decimation of more than 15.6 million acres. Fires can be started by lightning strikes. They can also be ignited accidentally or deliberately by a spark.

Read Proverbs 16:27 and fill in the blank. *A worthless man digs up evil, while his words are like scorching* _____.

The footnote in the *New King James Version, Personal Study Bible* further explains that people who use words to start a verbal fire are *ungodly, perverse, and violent.*[39] How do our tongues, either accidentally or deliberately, start a fire?

A spark from our tongue can kill a relationship, ruin a reputation, and destroy our Christian witness. When we shine the light on our hurtful words, we discover that words can ignite a fire within someone's heart that leaves lifetime scars.

Friends, we don't want to be the reason for someone else's scars. We want to get control of our mouth. Read Proverbs 15:2 and Proverbs 16:23. What do both of these verses say about a person who holds their tongue?

Recall James 1:5. God will provide wisdom so we can use our words in the right way. Even within Christian circles, we can talk in an unedifying way. The Bible reveals the underlying problem for when this happens.

Read the following Scriptures and underline the reason behind our lack of control.

Proverbs 4:23: *Watch over your heart with all diligence, for from it flow the springs of life.* (or death, depending the Bible version)

Luke 6:45: *The good man out of the good treasure of his heart brings forth what is good; and the evil man out of the evil treasure brings forth what is evil; for his mouth speaks from that which fills his heart.*

Matthew 12:34: *You brood of vipers, how can you, being evil, speak what is good? For the mouth speaks out of that which fills the heart.*

Brood of vipers — nest of deadly snakes. First introduced in the Garden of Eden, Satan was the personification of evil, disguised as a venomous snake. His lie brought destruction to all humanity.

Based on the previous three verses, what is the connection between the mouth and the heart?

God sees our heart and gives this warning in Ezekiel 11:21: *"As for those whose hearts go after their detestable things and abominations, I will bring their conduct down on their heads," declares the Lord GOD.* Wow! Conviction is heavy.

But God invites us to confess and repent of our sins (recall James chapter two). Repentance leads to forgiveness and results in freedom. We might ask ourselves how to get our mouths under control so that we don't continue to sin. King David suggested a solution in Psalm 39:1. What was his idea to avoid sin?

When and where do you most need to muzzle your mouth?

What do you think would happen if the people with whom you work and socialize prayed Psalm 39:1 before beginning the day?

Matthew 12:37 tells us this: *For every idle word I will have to give an account. My words will be judged – as either justified or condemned.* We have a choice. We can use our tongue as a weapon to bring destruction or as a weapon to strike down Satan's attempt to destroy a person's self-worth and purpose. We can also choose to speak life-giving words. Because we love God and want to obey Him, our words will reflect what's in our hearts. The Holy Spirit guides our speech and helps us put on the figurative muzzle. He also brings to our memory verses that empower us to show restraint.

The acronym T.H.I.N.K can be helpful too. Ask yourself if what you are about to say is:

> T - True
>
> H - Helpful
>
> I - Inspiring
>
> N - Necessary
>
> K - Kind

Recall Proverbs 12:18 quoted at the beginning of the lesson: *There is one who speaks rashly like the thrusts of a sword, but the tongue of the wise brings healing.* The NIV uses the word *reckless* in place of *rashly*. To be reckless means to act without thinking or caring about the consequences. Synonyms include hasty, negligent, thoughtless, brash. But look closely at the conclusion of this wisdom verse: A wise tongue brings healing.

Additionally, Proverbs 10:19 tells us *when there are many words, transgression is unavoidable, but he who restrains his lips is wise.* Other Bible translations use these words in place of restrains: *spares, few, controls. Merriam-Webster* defines restraint like this: "to prevent from doing, exhibiting, or expressing something; to limit, restrict, or keep under control."[40]

A wise person restrains, muzzles, hurtful words from bursting forth yet permits healing words to freely flow. And where does wisdom come from? A transformed heart begins the wisdom process, and a wise person submits to God for direction — a beautiful cycle that enables us to use our mouth for God's glory.

Prayer

God, help me know

- what to do.
- what to say.
- what to think.
- where to go.

For Reflection

What did God reveal about His character?

How have you been challenged in a specific area of your life?

How will you apply the passage to your daily routine?

How is your faith being strengthened?

Ж

It doesn't make sense to curb what our culture says is normal to blurt out, but the Holy Spirit empowers us with self-control and restraint.

Ж

Godly Friends Chime In

CAROL recalls, "We were preparing to move to Montana when my husband suddenly passed away. I finished up my last year of teaching in California so I could retire. Church services were very hard, especially the music. Standing in His presence, the loss was overwhelming. I heard a whisper and felt a hand touching mine as I gripped the pew in front of me. It was Grayce whom I had known for several years but since we lived in different towns church functions were our only common bond. On that day that changed. The Lord sent Grayce, a lovely lady who had lost her husband years before, to comfort and encourage me. May we each be able to provide that godly comfort to another."

SHERRY says, "I was reminded of the time I was a leader in AWANAs. We memorized Isaiah 53:7: *He was oppressed, and He was afflicted, yet He opened not his mouth; like a lamb that is led to the slaughter, and like a sheep that before it's shearers is silent, so He opened not his mouth.* I want to be the kind of person who knows when to speak and when to remain quiet. That's why the T.H.I.N.K acronym is especially meaningful to me."

Week 3, Day 3

The Choice Is Ours

Read James 3:6–8:

The tongue is a fire, the very world of iniquity; the tongue is set among our members as that which defiles the entire body, and sets on fire the course of our life, and is set on fire by hell. For every species of beasts and birds, of reptiles and creatures of the sea, is tamed and has been tamed by the human race but no one can tame the tongue; it is a restless evil and full of deadly poison.

*H*ere we go again.

Maybe James' group was hardheaded. He reiterated to his circle of Christian friends the serious destruction that proceeds from a spark — the hot flame of the tongue. *It's human nature,* some say, *the gift of gab we receive just by being born.* True. But we can choose how we want to use (or unleash) this gift.

In our passage today, circle the words *tongue* (v. 6), *defiles* (v. 6), *evil* (v. 8), and *deadly poison* (v. 8). As we return to the "brood of vipers spewing deadly poison," we might all decide we'd rather clean the bathroom. At least the bathroom is tangible, and cleaning it is something we can control.

When we've lost control of our tongue and our flesh takes over, our natural, selfish tendencies surface. In this case, the tongue is described as defiling, evil, and full of deadly poison. Various translations say the tongue stains or corrupts, but most translations use he term deadly poison in their description of the tongue. A rhetorical question, for sure, but which of the following has the potential to poison another person? Circle all that apply.

Lying	Gossip	Exaggeration
Slander	Criticism	Sarcasm
Idle talk	Abusive speech	Mean-spirited conversation

Deadly poison kills the physical body; harmful words kill the soul.

Let's go deeper. Ephesians 4:29 tells us: *Let no unwholesome word proceed from your mouth, but only such a word as is good for edification according to the need of the moment, so that it will give grace to those who hear.*

The Greek word translated unwholesome is *sapros*. It means rotten.[41] The ESV and KJV use the word *corrupt*, and the RSV uses *evil*. The NLT renders the verse this way: *Don't use foul or abusive language. Let everything you say be good and helpful, so that your words will be an encouragement to those who hear them.*

Circle the words *foul* and *abusive*. Abusive language is a form of emotional abuse. Think about the definitions of these words:

Abusive: Using harsh, insulting language . . . emotional cruelty.

Foul: Offensive, obscene, abusive, detestable, vulgar or insulting language.[42]

For some, using foul language is a habit. Maybe they grew up with this type of language in the home or live in a culture where this kind of language is socially acceptable. Do you struggle in these areas? Why or why not?

In what ways have we become numb to or accepting of our culture's use of foul language?

Can a foul mouth detract from a Christian's witness? Why or why not?

Can sarcasm be hurtful dialogue? Why or why not?

Do you think gossip qualifies as a form of abuse? Why or why not?

Match each of the following references to its best summary.

    ____ Proverbs 11:13   A. A gossip reveals secrets.

    ____ Proverbs 20:19   B. Gossipers are busybodies.

    ____ 1 Timothy 5:13   C. Avoid people who gossip.

In James 3:2–5, we read how talking too much can lead to sin. Is it possible for a person to participate in gossip without saying a word? If so, how?

Spurgeon said, "If there were no gratified hearers of ill reports, there would be an end to the trade of spreading them."[43] Ouch!

We need to put gossip to death. What else needs to be buried with gossip? Recall Colossians 3:8–9 tells us: *Now you also, put them all aside: anger, wrath, malice, slander, and abusive speech from your mouth. Do not lie to one another, since you laid aside the old self with its evil practice.*

Those verses contain a list of destructive sins. Zero in on *slander.* The Greek word translated here as "slander" is *diaboloi.* Interestingly, it is from the root word for devil.[44] It describes a person who is an "accuser, defamer, [and] those who maliciously attack another's good name, humiliate or malign others. They speak falsehoods for the purpose of damaging others.

What are the other sins listed in Colossians 3:8–9?

Ephesians 4:31 reiterates: *Let all bitterness and wrath and anger and clamor and slander be put away from you, along with all malice.* Both lists contain sins that emerge from a hostile heart and could burst forth and spew from the mouth.

Return to the rhetorical question. With what area(s) do you struggle the most?

James says, "No one can tame the tongue." Why do you think this could be considered good news?

The Holy Spirit dwells within us and empowers us to live according to God's commandments. God is the only One who changes hearts. The good news is that He never meant for us to struggle on our own, and He has provided the Holy Spirit to help us gain control of our tongues.

Used in the right way, our tongue is a powerful tool that can bring life to the emotionally dead.

Proverbs 15:1–4 tells us *a gentle answer turns away wrath, but a harsh word stirs up anger. The tongue of the wise makes knowledge acceptable, but the mouth of fools spouts folly. The eyes of the Lord are in every place, watching the evil and the good. A soothing tongue is a tree of life, but perversion in it crushes the spirit.*

At first glance, Proverbs 15:3 — *the eyes of the Lord are in every place* — appears out of place. But the verse is a fitting reminder that God hears the way we choose to speak. Two different uses for our language are described: one is wicked, the other good.

Compare these two uses by listing the descriptive words from Proverbs 15:1–4 in the appropriate columns.

      Wicked: Good:

Return to Ephesians 4:29. List the kinds of words that bring life to those who hear.

Think back on a time you made a big bowl of popcorn and salted it. Why did you add salt? What did the salt do to the popcorn?

What does Colossians 4:6 tell us our speech needs to be seasoned with? Why?

Salt is essential for life; it's one of the oldest and most common seasonings and preservatives. As a preservative, it prevents decay. As a seasoning it adds flavor.

Our mouths have amazing potential to bring life:

Proverbs 12:25: *Anxiety in a man's heart weighs it down, but a good word makes it glad.*

Proverbs 15:23: *A man has joy in an apt answer, and how delightful is a timely word!*

Proverbs 16:24: *Pleasant words are as a honeycomb, sweet to the soul, and health to the bones.*

Proverbs 31:26: *She opens her mouth in wisdom, and the teaching of kindness is on her tongue.*

Notes

As we mature in our relationship with God, we'll be better able to use our words to bring health, healing, and life. May Psalm 19:14 always be our prayer: *Let the words of my mouth and the meditation of my heart be acceptable in Your sight, O Lord, my rock and my Redeemer.*

Who can you bring life to today?

Prayer

God, help me know

- what to do.
- what to say.
- what to think.
- where to go.

For Reflection

What did God reveal about His character?

How have you been challenged in a specific area of your life?

How will you apply the passage to your daily routine?

How is your faith being strengthened?

✕

It doesn't make sense to abstain from using language that is socially acceptable, but by the Holy Spirit's power, our mouths become a wellspring of life.

✕

Godly Friends Chime In

MEG says, "Wow, I'm reminded of throwing a rock into a lake. It becomes a ripple effect and has widespread impact for either positive or negative. It made me think further: If rocks create a ripple effect, and Jesus is our Rock (Psalm 19:14), then the impact will be great!"

SHERRY reacts, "The tongue, oh, the tongue! Using sarcastic words aren't as innocent as I thought. My words don't just affect the person I say them to; they also 'stain my whole body.' I am diligently working on being aware and careful of the words I use."

DEBBIE admits, "I admit wearing a mask during the COVID-19 Pandemic for the purpose of maintaining good physical health helped me visualize wearing a mask like a muzzle to hold in my inappropriate words for the sake of our emotional health!"

Week 3, Day 4

The Double Life

Read James 3:9–12:

With it we bless our Lord and Father, and with it we curse men, who have been made in the likeness of God; from the same mouth come both blessing and cursing. My brethren, these things ought not to be this way. Does a fountain send out from the same opening both fresh and bitter water? Can a fig tree, my brethren, produce olives, or a vine produce figs? Nor can salt water produce fresh.

A person who speaks well of God, openly praising Him, but who also verbally abuses or mistreats another person sends a confusing message. Who or what is confusing? Is it the message itself or the person? Explain.

When have you been perplexed about a person's talk that didn't match her walk . . . or vise versa?

James 1:8 uses the word *double-minded,* which comes from the Greek word *dipsuchos,* meaning "a person with two minds or souls."[45] This is important to our understanding of a double-minded person: The condition of our heart and mind is the motivation for what we say and do. Our philosophy, convictions, persuasions, values, and principles drive our behavior. In fact, our actions reflect what we believe about God, our identity in Him, His purpose for us, and our mission on earth. If our mind is unclear, ambiguous, weak, or easily persuaded, then our behavior will be also.

How can what we say reveal with whom we associate?

How can what we do divulge with whom we spend time?

Look at these examples of conflicting talk and action:

In the morning, with one group, **we thank** God for His mercy and forgiveness. By evening, though, we withhold mercy from others.

On Sunday, **we worship** God, then on Monday we worship ourselves when we insist on having our own way.

On Tuesday, **we gather** with our evening church group to discuss our love for each other, then on Wednesday at work, we gossip and slander a co-worker who's absent.

On Thursday, **we read** in the Bible about the true freedom that comes from extending forgiveness, but on Friday we refuse to forgive an offender.

On Saturday, **we say** we love God and desire to obey Him, yet on Saturday night we hold back when God says to be generous with our money and care for others.

You get the idea.

A double-minded person lives life on a spiritual roller coaster. Her ever-changing speech and behaviors are confusing. She can't make up her mind as to what she believes. Onlookers wonder, *Is she for God, or against Him?* What do you call people who behave this way?

We may label a person as a *faker, two-faced, pretender*, but as I've learned from hanging out with the teens, *poser*, also fits.

These descriptions are unappealing, and most of us wouldn't want to be labeled by them. But James addresses the issue because first-century Christians were riding the poser rollercoaster. *Are we?* When are you most likely to flip-flop in your beliefs?

Today's passage opened with the words "with it," continuing the discussion from previous passages about the tongue's proper and improper use. Then, almost in an unexpected way, James boldly asserts that we bless God with our mouth, yet we curse others. We thank God for our blessings, then behave as if we're dissatisfied. This is incongruent behavior.

Let's focus on the first part. What do you think it means to *bless God?*

Piper writes, "My thesis is that in the Scripture when God 'blesses' men they are thereby helped and strengthened and made better off than they were before, but when men 'bless' God He is not helped or strengthened or made better off. Rather, man's blessing God is an 'expression of praising thankfulness.' It is an 'exclamation of gratitude and admiration.'"[46]

Do you express gratitude and admiration for God only on certain times and days, or is thankfulness a regular occurrence?

Why do you think people outside of the church call people within the church hypocrites? On what do you think they base that judgment?

What is the difference between being real and being a hypocrite — an imposter or pretender?

James explains how opposing behavior is nonsense — even baffling. He uses three analogies — all opposites. Reread James 3:10–12, identify these analogies, and fill in the missing words.

Can a _____ send forth _____ and _____? (v.11)

Can a _____ bear _____ _____? (v. 12)

Can a _____ bear _____ _____? (v. 12)

Why do you think humans are influenced or drawn to a contradictory lifestyle?

There are various reasons for a double-minded lifestyle. Let's ask ourselves some personal questions to help us get to the source.

Am I a people pleaser? If so, how can this mindset contribute to changing viewpoints or ideas?

Do I exaggerate or drop names to build myself up or appear to be popular or prestigious? If yes, what circumstances prompt this behavior?

Does fear of being opposed cause me to go along with the group even when following is unhealthy or sets a bad example? If yes, what group encourages that behavior?

Do I criticize other people before they have a chance to condemn me? If yes, explain what situations usually generate your criticism.

Do I agree or laugh with others so they'll like me? If so, where is the most likely place for this to happen?

Am I too timid to show my faith? If yes, what makes me most afraid?

Am I swayed by others? If yes, when is that most likely to occur?

The answers to these questions may suggest we're motivated by fear — fear of defeat, fear of criticism, and fear of exclusion, even by our church group. Ultimately, the fear is a self-esteem issue. The answer to low self-esteem, however, isn't high self-esteem. It's esteem in and through God — seeing ourselves through God's eyes as someone who is beloved, capable, enough.

Like everything else we've studied or will ever study in God's Word, whatever we think or do is connected to the heart. When our heart is divided or confused, our behavior will be, too. Just as we cannot mix salt water with fresh water and produce only fresh water or only salt water, neither should we exemplify inconsistent, double standards with thoughts or beliefs that flip flop depending on the people we're with or the situation we're in.

The church is — or should be — a place where God's people gather to worship. Why do you think we have trouble being real in this atmosphere?

How might we unknowingly contribute to harming another believer?

In James 2 we learned about the evidence — the fruit of the Spirit — of God in our life. What would your friends, family, and co-workers, say is evident in your life? Do they know where you stand?

In the long run, a confusing, wishy-washy, back-and-forth lifestyle will leave us not only exhausted, but also defeated. Let's ask God to help us live a consistent lifestyle.

Prayer

God, help me know

- what to do.
- what to say.
- what to think.
- where to go.

For Reflection

What did God reveal about His character?

Ж

It doesn't make sense that although we live in a fake society, we can live a consistent lifestyle that demonstrates our single devotion to God.

Ж

How have you been challenged in a specific area of your life?

How will you apply the passage to your daily routine?

How is your faith being strengthened?

Godly Friends Chime In

SHELIA shares a memory. "When the recession of 2008 happened, my faith was really put to the test. Honestly, I couldn't remember a time that I didn't trust God; it was in my nature. I have always been pretty consistent about God's faithfulness in all situations. Yet, suddenly I found myself questioning if God saw the mess we were in and if He was going to rescue us. Since trusting God came so easily for me, I was shaken and surprised by my fear and questioned what had changed.

I turned to my Father and confessed that I had been temporarily overcome with a lack of faith. All things did work out in His timing and my God was faithful. But the greatest lesson for me is how easy it is to have two mindsets. Since then, my daily prayer is to trust Him only — no matter what happens."

SHERRY also reflects on a season when she behaved one way, but had opposing thoughts. "In 1995, our family was less than two months away from celebrating my husband's six-year kidney transplant anniversary. Then suddenly, life took an unexpected turn. My husband was once again in the midst of a health crisis . . . cancer.

During my husband's first chemotherapy treatment he was overdosed with the equivalent of two chemo treatments, which made him deathly sick, and put him in the hospital. Shortly thereafter, we were informed by his kidney doctor that the anti-rejection medicine needed to keep his body from rejecting the transplanted kidney, was allowing the cancer to spread throughout his lymph nodes, abdomen, and liver, so it would have to be discontinued. As a result, he would most likely lose the kidney.

I would love nothing more than to tell you that I put my total trust in God and never wavered, but that wouldn't be the truth. I felt defeated. My outward facade was that I was completely trusting God. But inwardly, I was filled with doubt and instability. Graciously, the Holy Spirit kept reminding me of God's promise to carry my burden. One day I knelt before God and genuinely told Him I would trust Him and accept His will.

We learned that the kidney God had provided six-years earlier was a perfect match and he no longer needed any anti-rejection medicine. God blessed us with a tremendous testimony of His faithfulness and a more consistent trusting attitude."

Week 3, Day 5

Biblical Wisdom

Read James 3:13–18:

> *Who among you is wise and understanding? Let him show by his good behavior his deeds in the gentleness of wisdom. But if you have bitter jealousy and selfish ambition in your heart, do not be arrogant and so lie against the truth. This wisdom is not that which comes down from above, but is earthly, natural, demonic. For where jealousy and selfish ambition exist, there is disorder and every evil thing. But the wisdom from above is first pure, then peaceable, gentle reasonable, full of mercy and good fruits, unwavering, without hypocrisy. And the seed whose fruit is righteousness is sown in peace by those who make peace.*

*M*ason (the boy I told you about when we discussed James 1:5) said, "We're wise when we use our experiences to impact people in good ways." I think Mason is smarter than I was as a child. Back then I thought we automatically became wise as we aged. I pictured wisdom as a lightbulb and thought it turned on automatically when we aged.

What do you think? How does a woman become spiritually mature and wise?

You may recall what was said in Week 1, Day 3 of our study: If an older woman chooses to leave God out of her daily life, she remains unchanged by Him. A younger woman, however, who spends time in the Word of God, finds truth and wisdom. She is able to produce Christ-like conduct because of the Holy Spirit dwelling within her.

Recall also the definition of *knowledge* and *wisdom*.

Knowledge is "information gained through experience, reasoning, or acquaintance."

Wisdom is "the ability to discern or judge what is true, right, or lasting."[47]

Think about an older intelligent woman you personally know. What traits or characteristics reveal her knowledge? For example, do you know she's knowledgeable based on the work she does or her extensive vocabulary? Explain.

Now think about another woman you consider to be wise. How is her wisdom evidenced?

In what ways do these two women differ?

Who is a younger woman that you would describe as wise?

Read 1 Corinthians 1:20–21. Based on this passage, is there wisdom in this world? Where does this wisdom take us — or not take us?

Read on to 1 Corinthians 1:25 and discover that the world's wisdom is foolishness to God.

Wiersbe, compares the earth's wisdom to God's wisdom in this adapted chart: [48]

The World's Wisdom	God's Wisdom
Envy; self-promotion; selfishness; human glorification	Motivated to point others to God and show His glory.
Strife; seeks approval from others; asks if others are for you or against you; rivalry; division	Humility; esteems others.
Boastful; proud	Resists urge to compare oneself to others.
Deceitful	Seeks truth in God's Word and brings to light the hidden things in darkness.
Meekness is seen as weakness Selfishly asserts self	Self-controlled; seeks to honor God; seeks His wisdom.
Worldliness; sinful life; spiritual adulterer	Pure and holy because God is holy.
Competition; rivalry; war; denies or covers up sin	Peace; purity in life results in peace; confesses sin.
Provokes others; blames; causes fights	Reasonable; truthful; gentle
Hard to get along with; stubborn	Agreeable; easy to live and work with.
Withholds mercy; gives others "what they deserve"	Shows mercy without expecting gain.
Striving; empty life	Faithful, full life; practical; produces good works.
Wavers; gives in to pressures; changes viewpoint; fearful	Unchanging; single minded; decisive; strong; courageous.
Hypocritical; insincere; pretense; hiding	Open; honest

Notes

How would you summarize the difference between God's wisdom and man's wisdom?

Revering God is wise and brings a victorious life on earth and eternal life in heaven. What this world offers leads to dissatisfaction, defeat, and death.

Imagine an elaborate staircase between two columns that ascend upward. In your helplessness you run up those stairs and into the arms of your Heavenly Father. That is a picture of wisdom.

Go ahead, girl. Run up that staircase. God is waiting to receive you!

Prayer

God, help me know

- what to do.
- what to say.
- what to think.
- where to go.

For Reflection

What did God reveal about His character?

How have you been challenged in a specific area of your life?

How will you apply the passage to your daily routine?

How is your faith being strengthened?

Ж

It doesn't make sense, but wisdom is obtainable — at any age — for any person who turns to God.

Ж

Godly Friends Chime In

SHERRY says, "Oh how I love the visual of running up the staircase to Father God for help! Visualizing this, gave me goose bumps and a ray of sunshine in my heart."

DEBBIE shares, "I was seeking wisdom to know whether or not I should confront another Christian who didn't keep his word. I was so surprised when God whispered to my heart so quickly and emphatically, *It doesn't matter whether you choose to confront or not. What matters is your reaction and attitude. If you confront, but not in love, then don't do it. And if you choose not to confront, but hold a grudge and are bitter, that's wrong too.* It made so much sense. Well, of course it did. It was the wisdom of God. God will always discipline and judge us, and others, fairly. What I needed to be concerned with the most wasn't if I *should* but rather *how* my attitude is while doing it."

Truths from James 3

- God sees a person's heart.
- The tongue is a powerful weapon.
- The tongue can speak encouragement.
- The mouth is the outflow of the heart.
- The tongue has the potential to bring spiritual death or life.
- We produce what we are made of.
- Seek godly wisdom.
- Avoid earthly wisdom.
- Friendship with the world means accepting its ideals.
- Friendship with the world is in opposition to God.
- Do not use the tongue for evil.
- Be of one conviction for Christ — not double-minded.
- Having knowledge is not the same as having wisdom.
- Humility brings us to God.
- Wisdom begins with knowing, fearing, and respecting God.
- Conviction may feel like a heavy burden.
- Conviction leads to repentance.
- Repentance leads to God's forgiveness.
- We're influential within our community.
- Sometimes we're quiet learners.
- Sometimes we speak as master teachers.
- A transformed heart is the first step toward wisdom.
- Wisdom transforms the heart.

Week 4, Day 1

God Is Faithful . . . Are We?

Read James 4:1–5:

What is the source of quarrels and conflicts among you? Is not the source your pleasures that wage war in your members? You lust and do not have; so you commit murder. You are envious and cannot obtain; so you fight and quarrel. You do not have because you do not ask. You ask and do not receive, because you ask with wrong motives, so that you may spend it on your pleasures. You adulteresses, do you not know that friendship with the world is hostility toward God? Therefore whoever wishes to be a friend of the world makes himself an enemy of God. Or do you think that the Scripture speaks to no purpose: "He jealously desires the Spirit which He has made to dwell in us"?

> While sifting through the challenges that accompanied my husband's battle with cancer, I called out to God with many questions about this dark, difficult time. Sometimes I used words; other times all I had were tears. But in my search for direction, God answered with a gentle tug on my heart: I'm not asking for your permission; I'm asking you to be faithful.
>
> That's the moment everything changed for me. I had a new perspective — God's perspective — and I finally understood what God is calling me to do during this season of our lives.

Each of us has a unique purpose. All of us are called to be faithful. I wonder, though, if God is faithful to His people, what could it mean for me to be faithful to Him?

Being unfaithful or disloyal are often used as synonyms for adultery, but a person can also be disloyal to an employer. To be called an adulteress is a strong accusation — one that most of us wouldn't use to describe our faithlessness or indifference to God. In today's passage, James confronted his Christian brothers and sisters for their unfaithful behavior.

The Greek word for adulteress is *moichalis*. God's intimate alliance with the people of Israel was like a marriage. When they reverted into idolatry, God accused them of committing adultery or playing the harlot.[48] James charged the Christ-followers with this same kind of spiritual adultery.

Who were the Christians committing adultery against?

What do you think it means to be faithful to God?

When we made the decision to follow Jesus Christ, we probably never considered the possibility of committing spiritual adultery. The choice to follow Jesus was, in fact, the first step in becoming a faithful follower. Yet, to remain faithful requires intentionality.

To be faithful to God means:

- We give our devotion to Him alone. We refuse to look to another entity to find significance, worth, or love. First Kings 8:61 tells us this: *Let your heart therefore be wholly devoted to the LORD our God, to walk in His statutes and to keep His commandments, as at this day.*

- We depend on His strength alone for every task we undertake. We also depend on Him to help us with each emotion that floods our heart. Nehemiah 8:10 tells us *the joy of the Lord is your strength.*

- We spend time with Him by reading His Word. Jeremiah 15:16 tells us: *Your words were found and I ate them. And Your words became for me a joy and the delight of the heart.*

- We wait expectantly for God to act. In Romans 12:12 we read: *Rejoice in our confident hope. Be patient in trouble, and keep on praying.*

- We talk with Him. We wouldn't ignore our best friend. Neither should we ignore God. Through prayer, we create intimacy and a personal relationship with Him. Psalm 145:18–19 tells us: *The Lord is near to all who call upon Him, to all who call upon Him in truth. He will fulfill the desire of those who fear Him; He will also hear their cry and will save them.*

When we're faithful to God, we can expect the unexpected — joy! Not the happiness that's based on emotions and fluctuates as our situation does, but genuine joy that comes from believing God's Word, trusting He has a plan, and certain that He faithfully abides with us.

Sometimes, though, we're unfaithful. Our selfish desires surface and take precedence over what God desires for us. We search for other ways to have our needs met. Exodus 34:14 tells us God becomes jealous when that happens: *You shall not worship any other god, for the Lord, whose name is Jealous, is a jealous God.*

Let's clarify. Exodus 34:14 tells us not to do what?

And why?

First, an idol is anything that's more important than God. What are some potential idols in our culture?

Second, God is described as jealous. The definition of jealousy is "hostile toward one believed to enjoy an advantage."[50]

Read the following passages. How does the jealousy described in
Galatians 5 differ from the jealousy described in Exodus 20?

Galatians 5:20–21: *Idolatry, sorcery, enmities, strife, jealousy, outbursts of
anger, disputes, dissensions, factions, envying, drunkenness, carousing, and
things like these, of which I forewarn you, just as I have forewarned you,
that those who practice such things will not inherit the kingdom of God.*

Exodus 20:4–5: *You must not make for yourself an idol of any
kind or an image of anything in the heavens or on the earth or in
the sea. You must not bow down to them or worship them, for I,
the Lord your God, am a jealous God who will not tolerate your
affection for any other gods. I lay the sins of the parents upon
their children; the entire family is affected – even children in the
third and fourth generations of those who reject me* (NLT).

In Galatians 5:20 jealousy is listed among other sins. We're being
warned to avoid the discontentment and longing for something
that doesn't belong to us.

In Exodus 20, the freed Israelites made idols and worshipped
them instead of giving their worship to God. God's jealousy isn't
motivated by what He doesn't have, for He has everything. He is
jealous *for* us! He desires relationship with what is already His.

Wow! God wants what's His.

Have you given God a reason to be jealous?

Have you made anything more important than God?

Has any person become your god?

FIRST JOHN 2:15 TELLS US, *Do not love the world nor the things in the world. If anyone loves the world, the love of the Father is not in him.*

How can friendship with "the world" be spiritual adultery?

In this context, *befriending or loving the world* isn't about a person. To befriend the world means that we embrace worldly ideologies and accept earthly wisdom. A worldly perspective — or friendship with the world — is in opposition to God. If this happens, we've become unfaithful to the One who loves us and the One whom we say we love.

Piper puts it this way: "When we are told *not* to love the world, the Bible is referring to the world's corrupt value system. Loving the world means being devoted to the world's treasures, philosophies, and priorities. God tells His children to set their priorities according to His eternal value system."[51]

First Corinthians 15:33 warns: *Bad company corrupts good character.* Loving people doesn't mean becoming comfortable with an immoral society.

When we love God and commit ourselves to Him, we remain faithful and fulfill the first command to love God. This love for God motivates and enables us to love others. Piper continues, "The reason you shouldn't love the world is that you can't love the world and God at the same time. Love for the world pushes out love for God, and love for God pushes out love for the world."

Living in community (and in a secular culture) requires that we be interactive with others. Are there any situations that put you in a compromising position? If so, how will you handle that?

Is anything in our secular culture luring you away from God?

Wiersbe writes, "Friendship leads to loving the world and this makes it easy to conform to the world."[52] If we love God, then we don't want conform to ideologies that conflict with His Word. Look at these examples:

- You're watching a drama. The woman in an adulterous affair appears to be having fun, wrapped up in the romance of a new or mysterious love. You become envious, wishing your own husband could be that romantic.

- You're viewing a commercial, but the intended message is missed because you're focused on the exceptional home filled with an array of appliances and expensive décor. You deserve that too, and regardless of the cost, you won't be satisfied until you get it.

- You're watching a reality TV show, and the women laugh as they talk negatively about someone. Gossip seems funny, harmless — nothing to feel guilty about.

What are some practical ways to maintain your devotion to God?

Look back at James 4:1–5. Circle the following words and phrases: *quarrels, pleasures, lust, envious, you do not have,* and *wrong motives.* Consistent faithfulness to God minimizes these desires, whereas devotion to oneself accentuates the desire to have what's not yours or to get your way. How can a faithful relationship with Jesus diminish your desire to commit the sins you circled?

The following Scriptures can help:

- Psalm 133:1 says, *Behold, how good and how pleasant it is for brothers to dwell together in unity!* When we're devoted to God, quarrels are less frequent or more easily resolved. Appropriate boundaries are established.

- Psalm 20:4 says, ***May He grant you according to your heart's desire, and fulfill all your purpose*** (NKJV). Pleasures, or our desires, take a back seat to His desires for us.

- First Peter 2:11 tells us, ***Beloved, I urge you as aliens and strangers to abstain from fleshly lusts which wage war against the soul..*** Lust and envy are replaced with contentment.

- Hebrews 13:6 reminds us, *THE LORD IS MY HELPER, I WILL NOT BE AFRAID. WHAT WILL MAN DO TO ME?* Self-sufficiency is replaced with a dependency on God.

Quarrels, envy, and wrong motives have the potential to rob us of joy each day. Thankfully, God has told us to come to Him in repentance and He will forgive. Recall Psalm 51:10 which says, ***Create in me a clean heart, O God, and renew a steadfast spirit within me.*** When God cleanses our heart, we return to a right relationship with Him as a faithful child, devoted to Him alone — one who willingly runs to her Father to meet her every need.

To whom are you running today?

Prayer

God, help me know

- what to do.
- what to say.
- what to think.
- where to go.

For Reflection

What did God reveal about His character?

How have you been challenged in a specific area of your life?

How will you apply the passage to your daily routine?

How is your faith being strengthened?

Ж

*It doesn't make
sense to be faithful
to God whom we've
never seen, yet
His faithfulness
to us enables us to
develop an intimate
relationship with
Him that enables us
to shine.*

Ж

Godly Friends Chime In

JUDY admits, "I've got to say, having to be removed from my daily routines [per stay-at-home-order during the pandemic], I was reminded that I do place a lot of value on the things of this world that can be taken away in an instant! The constant thing is God and His great love for us."

JAMIE agrees, "It is so easy to succumb to the ways of the world. I sometimes don't realize that I'm allowing myself to be influenced by worldly views and I'm so grateful to my heavenly Father's gentle guidance back to His Word and desire for my life."

SAVANNAH chimes in, "This chapter was packed full of Aha! moments. First, I am reminded of 1 Corinthians 10:21 that says, *You cannot drink the cup of the Lord and the cup of demons; you cannot partake of the table of the Lord and the table of demons.* One foot in the world and one foot in God's kingdom is a lukewarm believer — half in and half out. God wants all of me!"

CINDY chimes in, "I feel close to God when He wakes me up in the middle of the night for no apparent reason. One night I felt led to ask God who I should be praying for since I was awake. He gave me a name and I prayed for that person. I now do this routinely when I find myself awake at night. After I pray for the person or people the Lord put on my heart, I am then usually able to go right back to sleep.

Week 4, Day 2

Drawing Close

Read James 4:6–10:

He gives a greater grace. Therefore it says, "GOD IS OPPOSED TO THE PROUD, BUT GIVES GRACE TO THE HUMBLE." Submit therefore to God. Resist the devil and he will flee from you. Draw near to God and He will draw near to you. Cleanse your hands, you sinners; and purify your hearts, you double-minded. Be miserable and mourn and weep; let your laughter be turned into mourning and your joy to gloom. Humble yourselves in the presence of the Lord, and He will exalt you.

You don't have to imagine a pandemic if you're school-aged and above in 2020.

But imagine this scene: You're taking a walk with a friend; your voices are anxious and questions about COVID-19 are flying. You're fully engaged in what is taking place in your immediate community. You and your friend discuss the political responses and the CDC's recommendations. You also debate what's real and what's fake. You share your disappointment about cancelled reunions, vacations, and weddings. Fear grips the unemployed. Parents and teachers are confused by unexpected educational changes. Then, with a squirt of hand sanitizer, you greet a third, somewhat familiar face. She joins you on your walk and joins the conversation.

She asks, "What's been going on?"

With a peculiar look, you ask, "Where have you been? It's all over the news." The three of you continue your walk, careful to abide by the six-feet social distance recommendation.

A similar scene occurred more than 2,000 years ago.

Two friends walked the road to Emmaus and discussed the granddaddy of all current events: the resurrection of Jesus Christ. Was it real? Was it fake? Was He God's son? The government insisted a robbery had occurred. Gossip swarmed through the city like killer bees. Suspicion was mounting against the disciples as the prime suspect for stealing the body. Christ-followers were in despair because their Savior had been killed. Many people ridiculed them.

Read the account in Luke 24:13–35.

What were the friends talking about? (Luke 24:14)

Who approached? (Luke 24:15)

What did Jesus ask? (Luke 24:17)

How did they respond to Jesus? (Luke 24:18)

Again, what did Jesus ask? (Luke 24:19)

Why were these friends disappointed? (Luke 24:21)

Return to your imaginary walk. The three of you decide to relax and fellowship in the vacant park — on separate benches, of course. And that's when it hits you. The familiar face of your unnamed friend is indeed someone you know — a former college professor. It had been a while since you had seen her face or heard her voice.

Now go back to the Road to Emmaus.

What did the friends and Jesus do to rest from their weary, dusty walk (Luke 24:28–30)?

After Cleopas and his companion spend quality time in fellowship with Jesus, something amazing happened. Luke 24:31 tells us that they finally recognized Jesus' voice! They knew Him.

In the COVID-19 pandemic of 2020, citizens were strongly urged to distance themselves from each other. But Jesus invites us to come close to Him.

Draw near. Move in. Walk with. What an amazing invitation from our heavenly Father.

Walking closely with God doesn't happen automatically; it requires intentionality on our part, just as cultivating any relationship would. A relationship with Jesus operates the same way — the more time we spend with God in Bible reading, prayer, worship, praise, and thanksgiving, the closer our relationship with Him becomes, and we're more attuned to His voice.

We've talked about this before. Spending time with Jesus is precious and special. Time with Him is never wasted. In fact, time with God is priceless and promises to transform our lives. So, when and where do you spend time with God?

When do you feel close to Him?

Describe a season in your life when you felt distant from God.

What changed between your closest time with God and your most distant time?

On a scale of 1–10 with 10 being the closest, how close do you feel to God today?

1   2   3   4   5   6   7   8   9   10

Micah 6:8 tells us, *He has told you, O man, what is good; and what does the LORD require of you but to do justice, to love kindness, and to walk humbly with your God?*

For many, the concept of "walking with God" is baffling. Simply defined, walking is a verb indicating a continuous movement and progression forward. In this context, walking is movement forward to discover the character of God and His will for our life.

Look back at Micah 6:8. What adverb makes it possible to walk closely with God?

James 4:6–10 clarifies what brings us close to Jesus versus what pushes us away: pride vs. humility; submission vs. resistance; and releasing sin vs. reveling in it.

To draw near to God:

1. Approach God in humility.

   To better understand what God is resisting and what He is giving, let's define these words:

   Pride: Showing a high or excessively high opinion of oneself or one's importance; deep pleasure or satisfaction as a result of one's own achievements, qualities, or possessions.[53]

   Humility: Freedom from arrogance.[54]

   Grace: The free and unmerited favor of God, as manifested in the salvation of sinners and the bestowal of blessings.[55]

   Pride puts distance between God and us.

   Read Psalm 138:6: *Though the Lord is on high, yet He regards the lowly; but the _____ He knows from afar.*

   Now read Psalm 25:9: *He leads the _____ in justice, and He teaches the _____ His way.*

   Some translations substitute the word *meek* or *mild* for *humble*. For clarification, to be humble, meek, or mild, doesn't mean that a person has a poor self-image or a lack of self-worth. Rather, a humble person recognizes her worth in God and His work in her.

2. Submit to God.

   The devil opposes God, and pride is one of the weapons he uses to entice Christians to oppose God also. Submission, however, enables us to resist the devil. And when we submit to God, the devil loses. Wiersbe explains: "The word [submit] is a military term that means 'get into proper order'"[56]

   What are the repercussions for when we get our priorities out of order?

Has there been a time that you did things your way? If so, what was the result?

What, if anything, do you need to submit to God? Are any of the following words applicable?

Competition	Fear	Control
Envy	Stubbornness	Criticism
Busyness	Other_____	

3. Confess our sins.

In Psalm 24:3–4 we read: *Who may ascend into the hill of the Lord? And who may stand in His holy place? He who has clean hands and a pure heart, who has not lifted up his soul to falsehood and has not sworn deceitfully.*

Circle *clean hands and a pure heart,* and *falsehood.* Confess sin to Jesus. Weep over it. Resist the urge to accept certain sins as less offensive to God than other sins. Confess all sin with genuine remorse.

Matthew Poole, a seventeenth century theologian, wrote, "A broken and a contrite heart is a heart deeply afflicted and grieved for sin, humbled under the sense of God's displeasure, and earnestly seeking and willing to accept reconciliation with God upon any terms."[57]

Read Psalm 34:18. To whom is the Lord near?

Barnes explained, "The phrase, 'them that are of a broken heart,' refers to a condition when a burden 'seems' to be on the heart, and when the heart 'seems' to be crushed by sin or sorrow; and it is designed to describe a consciousness of deep guilt, or the heaviest kind of affliction and trouble."[58]

A repentant heart is a broken heart. God moves close to the person who is sorry for her sin.

The friends on the road to Emmaus were discussing current events and didn't recognize Jesus until they moved closer into fellowship with him. During a pandemic we may need to distance ourselves from others, but it's imperative that we come close to Jesus.

Prayer

God, help me know

- what to do.
- what to say.
- what to think.
- where to go.

It doesn't make sense that the Ruler of Everything desires a closer relationship with us, but He tells us a relationship is exactly what He desires.

)(

For Reflection

What did God reveal about His character?

How have you been challenged in a specific area of your life?

How will you apply the passage to your daily routine?

How is your faith being strengthened?

Godly Friends Chime In

SAVANNAH says, "Yes, yes, yes! I just thought of something. Most of us are aware of the virus and how it shut down our economy. But are we that aware of God's presence?"

JAN shares, "Honestly, I know some people feel closer to God when things are going bad. But I have trouble hearing Him in bad times. I feel closer to God when things are going well. I praise Him, sing worship songs, read my Bible, and even pray harder. These are ways that I communicate with Him and it just draws me closer."

Criticism Versus Reproof

Read James 4:11–12:

> *Do not speak against one another, brethren. He who speaks against a brother or judges his brother, speaks against the law and judges the law; but if you judge the law, you are not a doer of the law but a judge of it. There is only one Lawgiver and Judge, the One who is able to save and to destroy; but who are you who judge your neighbor?*

*U*GH! Here we go again. More verses on using our words to discourage or hurt other Christians. James' group needs re-teaching. And judging? Yep, he talked about it in chapter two.

I thought I knew today's passage well. But now, using my NASB, I searched for what I thought was a missing word. Where was the word 'evil' that I remember from other translations? I huffed my breath in annoyance, then proceeded to read the passage in some other common translations.

Following are some of the most common Bible translations. There are others, but you'll get the idea. Emphasis is mine in all verses.

*Speak not **evil** one of another, **brethren**.* KJV

*Do not speak **evil** against one another, **brothers**.* ESV

*Do not speak **evil** of one another, **brethren**.* NKJV

*Don't speak **evil** against each other, dear **brothers and sisters**.* NLT

*Do not speak **against** one **another**.* NASB

*Brothers and sisters, do not **slander one another**.* NIV

*Don't **criticize and speak evil** about each other, dear **brothers**.* TLB

*Don't **bad-mouth** each other, **friends**.* MSG

In James 4:11–12, *evil* is synonymous with the words *against, slander, bad-mouth, criticize.* Let's remind ourselves. To whom is James writing? (Hint: His audience is in bold print, too.)

The phrase *evil speaking* is a translation of the Greek word *katalalia*; it means "to defame, to denigrate, to slander."[59] Put simply, evil speaking refers to the ease with which we toss insults, laugh while offending the listener, and appear innocent while smearing a fellow Christian's name. It's saying things about a person, her testimony, or her ministry that aren't helpful. This can include putting down an entire church.

Ouch! I've been criticized for my beliefs, and, sadly, I've criticized other Christians also.

Slander, as we studied in James chapter three, is making a false statement about someone . . . speaking words intended to hurt someone.

Anytime we speak to another person in a condescending way, our motivation shifts from helping someone to making ourselves look superior. Too often we tolerate discussing other Christians' weaknesses and finding fault with them. But by doing so, we're taking it on ourselves to judge God's people. In fact, to publicly put another Christian down is harmful to the entire body of Christ. The world is watching and listening. When they observe Christians arguing among themselves, they gain ammunition for their fight against Christianity.

Many years ago, a woman told me she could never be part of a certain Christian denomination. Maybe she had a bad experience at some time or another, but her criticism was against an entire denomination and against God's people.

God sees every Christian's ministry, church, or service. He alone knows their motivation for being in ministry and whether it's real or not. And He deals accordingly. In Psalm 120, King David protested against his accusers. David wasn't the first, and more than likely, we won't be the last to witness fault-finding and slander. God saw David's situation clearly; He sees ours too. When we do the right thing, God takes care of us. And when we don't, then God alone is our judge.

Just as the Bible teaches us to withhold criticism, it also explains that biblical correction is necessary. The difference between the two involves the motivation of our heart. Read 2 Timothy 4:2 in these different versions:

Preach the word; be ready in season and out of season; **reprove, rebuke, exhort,** *with great patience and instruction.* (NASB) (KJV) (ESV)

. . . **correct,** *rebuke and* **encourage** *— with great patience and careful instruction.* (NIV) (NLT)

. . . **convince,** *rebuke, exhort, with all longsuffering and teaching.* (NKJB) (RSV)

. . . correct, **confront,** *and encourage with patience and instruction.* (CEB)

Rebuke (or reprove) is used most often, followed by correct, exhort, convince and confront.

Barnes' Notes on the Bible clarifies rebuke: "In the New Testament the word is used to express a judgment of what is wrong or contrary to one's will, and hence, to admonish or reprove. It implies our conviction that there is something evil, or some fault in him who is rebuked. The word in this verse rendered "reprove," does not imply this, but merely that one may be in error, and needs to have arguments presented to convince him of the truth. That word also implies no superior authority in him who does it. He presents, "reasons, or argues" the case, for the purpose of convincing. The word here rendered rebuke, implies authority or superiority, and means merely that we may say that a thing is wrong, and administer a rebuke for it, as if there were no doubt that it was wrong.[60]

Similarly, the *Jamison Bible Commentary* defines reprove as [to] "convict, confute."[61]

We may be more familiar with the word *confrontation* than *rebuke* or *reproof.* From a secular perspective, "confrontation implies hostility, although like a fight, a confrontation can involve actual violence, or just a clash of words. It often refers to a military encounter involving opposing armies. This meaning became popular after the Cuban Missile Crisis in 1963. Before that, confrontation was used to mean "bringing two opposing parties face to face."[62]

Opposition and confrontation arise throughout God's Word. Confrontation, or the act of confronting, can be defined this way: "to face especially in challenge; oppose."[63]

Are you comfortable with confrontation, or do you choose to avoid it?

Do you actively steer clear of people with whom you might disagree? Why or why not?

What makes you more uncomfortable, confronting another or being confronted?

Regardless of whether we use rebuke, confront, oppose, or reprove, 2 Timothy 4:2 tells us how to approach a person with encouragement (exhortation), patience, instruction, or teaching.

Before confronting another person, however, consider the following six questions:

1. Have I established a caring relationship?

   Accountability between two people is based on a trusting, secure relationship with each other. It may not be possible to establish a relationship with someone we must correct or confront. But as a rule, confrontation is more effective when the person knows we're coming from a place of concern and care.

Think back to a time you were in a confrontation. Was there a confirmed relationship? Explain the outcome.

2. Have I prayed about this dilemma?

    When the need arises to correct a person, resist the urge to respond impulsively. Step back from the situation, take a deep breath, and pray first. Talking with another person about a sensitive subject, especially one that may provoke a defensive reaction, requires urgent prayer. In prayer, ask God to

    *   prepare the heart of the person you'll be confronting.

    *   provide you with understanding.

    *   give you the right words.

    *   go before you to establish His will.

3. Have I carefully chosen my words?

    Read 1 Timothy 4:13. Fill in the missing word. *Until I come, give attention to the public reading of Scripture, to _____ and teaching.*

    Most translations use the word exhortation. The Greek word *parakaleo,* translated as exhortation, means to "come alongside and help."[64] It involves comforting someone with strength and encouragement. Correction conveys the same idea. We come alongside a person to give counsel and show how the scriptures relate to the situation.

    In this way, how is encouragement related to confrontation?

    Read and summarize the following verses:

Galatians 6:1:

2 Timothy 2:25:

Based on those two verses, how should we approach any person who needs to be confronted or admonished?

Recall Proverbs 12:18: *There is one who speaks like the piercings of a sword, but the tongue of the wise promotes health.* Our goal must be to promote spiritual health and reconciliation to God.

4. Am I genuinely coming from a place of love for my fellow Christian?

   Confrontation should flow out of humility and a genuine desire to help another person move toward restoration. It shouldn't be a means of retaliation or motivated by an "I told you so" attitude.

   Second Timothy 2:23–24 says: *Don't have anything to do with foolish and stupid arguments, because you know they produce quarrels. And the Lord's servant must not be quarrelsome but must be kind to everyone, able to teach, not resentful.*

   What is the difference between a stupid argument and biblical correction?

   When we confront someone in love with the intent of restoration, then confrontation is not foolish. Confronting a person for a sinful attitude or behavior may be necessary for restoration or for their spiritual growth. From this perspective, confrontation, done properly, shows love.

5. Is this the right time?

    If God gives the green light and opens the door for correction to take place, He will show you the opportune time and optimal place. Meeting with a person after an extra-long, stressful day at work probably isn't the best time.

    Proverbs 27:14 tells us, *He who blesses his friend with a loud voice early in the morning, it will be reckoned a curse to him.* What do you think this verse implies?

    We can have the right words but when it's poor timing, we're more likely to be met with defensiveness.

6. Is confrontation always the right thing to do?

    Ask God if you should say anything at all. Not every person will respond or benefit from a confrontation, especially if there are other spiritual, emotional, or mental issues standing in the way or if the person doesn't understand what you're trying to convey. Jesus didn't waste time addressing every wrong action or thought. When the soldiers came to arrest Him in the Garden of Gethsemane, He didn't correct them or defend Himself (Matthew 26).

The message in James 4 is clear. Criticizing, putting another Christian down, smearing a person's name or ministry, is hurtful. But reproof — biblical correction or confrontation — is motivated by love with the intention to restore.

Prayer

God, help me know

- what to do.
- what to say.
- what to think.
- where to go.

For Reflection

What did God reveal about His character?

How have you been challenged in a specific area of your life?

How will you apply the passage to your daily routine?

How is your faith being strengthened?

Godly Friends Chime In

CAROL says, "Confronting peers is much more difficult for me than being confronted. It requires a clear mind rooted in God's Word without any obvious or hidden disgust or hostility when speaking to the offender. Love and reason should rule the entire conversation. This is why I agree that seeking the Lord's timing is so important."

SHERRY responds, "I'm comfortable confronting other people, but thankfully, it's not something I've done frequently. I can agree that it's been very obvious when a confrontation was guided by myself and not God! Argument and hurt feelings were the result."

Week 4, Day 4

Who Decides?

Read James 4:13–16

Come now, you who say, "Today or tomorrow we will go to such and such a city, and spend a year there and engage in business and make a profit." Yet you do not know what your life will be like tomorrow. You are just a vapor that appears for a little while and then vanishes away. Instead, you ought to say, "If the Lord wills, we will live and also do this or that." But as it is, you boast in your arrogance; all such boasting is evil.

*C*an you even begin to guesstimate how many decisions you make in a day? One source says that the average adult makes 35,000 decisions in a single day. That sounds like a crazy number! Maybe it is. Another source refutes this claim, stating that making this many decisions is impossible — we'd be making decisions every 1.5 seconds.[65] Forget the number. You know you make a ton of decisions.

My friend Cindy says that her day starts with simple decisions: What will I have for breakfast? Will I watch the news or sit in peace? Another cup of tea or is three enough?

But other decisions are life changing: choosing a career, selecting a school, determining the best course of action for health care, or making plans to sell/buy a home. Some decisions bring us joy, such as making arrangements for an annual vacation or choosing the right pet for the family. Others, though, are emotional battlegrounds as we determine how to fight for a prodigal child, a marriage, or job.

Important decisions may require advance planning and strategy, if time allows. Are you a planner or would you rather take things as they come — or one day at a time?

Organizational skills and the ability to plan are gifts from God that keep households and businesses afloat. James's chastisement wasn't because his readers made plans, but because they didn't seek God's will for their plans or decisions.

What about you? What decisions do you talk to the Lord about?

Which decisions do you consciously or unconsciously make on your own?

It seems reasonable that the more we communicate with God, the more clarity we'll have in our decision-making. And this is mostly true. Sometimes, however, we already know what to do. Let's break decision-making into three parts.

- Times we don't need to ask what to do
- Times we talk with God about a decision but His answer has less to do with the question than the answer
- Times we urgently cry out to God about decisions we're making

Let's get the first one out of the way. In some cases, we don't need to ask God what to do because He's told us already. (For example, we don't have to ask Him if we should manipulate others or retaliate against someone.) God has given us these answers in the Bible. So, the focus of our prayers in these cases shouldn't be what to do but rather how to go about it.

Second, sometimes God's fine with whichever way we go. For example, during a particular season after our kids were grown and moved out of the house, my husband and I considered selling our home and moving to another area. It was a reasonable thought, since I work from home, and Alan was nearing retirement. God wasn't calling us to move for a specific purpose. Rather, we were asking Him to grant our desire. I prayed for weeks and months about the move. Then one day while I was reading my Bible and praying, God whispered to my heart: *It's fine if you live in this house, and it's fine if you live in that one. What matters is that you are living a godly lifestyle and shining the light in the world — from this house or that house.*

Since we love to talk with God and consult Him about everything, the same principle applies to choosing one purse over another. Either purse is fine when you're responsible with the resources God has provided and carry your purse with a desire to be generous to other people. Only you know the answers to these personal questions.

Mostly, when making decisions like these, our conversation with God is about building a relationship with Him so His desires become our desires and what we desire is His will and purpose.

Third, we need to talk to God about our dreams, plans, visions, and passions. God has given these passions to us and invites us to partner with Him to bring them to fruition. But God also knows what's around the corner. Therefore, Proverbs 27:1 is especially meaningful: **Do not boast about tomorrow, for you do not know what a day may bring forth.** Make plans, but hold them loosely, because God may change them.

Life is brief when compared to eternity. Since we're not guaranteed tomorrow, we need to live each day fully and not waste the days we have. What is the difference between living a day on our own and living a day under the direction of God's leadership?

How can we invest in the kingdom of God and make an eternal impact?

Isaiah 40:6-8 put this truth into poetic form: *All flesh is grass, and all its loveliness is like the flower of the field. The grass withers, the flower fades, when the breath of the LORD blows upon it; surely the people are grass. The grass withers, the flower fades, but the word of our God stands forever.*

We all wither eventually, but the way we use our time and the decisions we make can make an everlasting difference. What can each of us do and say to have a life-changing impact on others, regardless of where we work or live?

We're wise when we realize the shortness of life and ask God to help us manage time wisely, invest in meaningful activities, and positively impact others. What is on your schedule for today?

We make plans. We seek God's help in decision-making. And we put God's will above our own. In reference to our schedule, we can pray: "God, here's the plan for the day. Give me strength to be productive and wisdom to discern Your will. But if You have plans for me to go in another direction, help me be flexible and maintain a good attitude."

What decisions are you currently making?

God is pleased when we pray His words back to Him. Here are some passages you can read or quote as you pray about decisions:

Trust in the Lord with all your heart and do not lean on your own understanding. In all your ways acknowledge Him, and He will make your paths straight. (Proverbs 3:5–6)

Circle "do not lean on your own understanding" and "acknowledge Him." Put a box around "He will make your paths straight." What is our responsibility? What is God's?

Your word is a lamp to my feet and a light to my path. Psalm 119:105

In what area do you need God to light up the path you should take?

Your ears will hear a word behind you, "This is the way, walk in it," whenever you turn to the right or to the left. Isaiah 30:21

What specific request are you waiting for God to answer?

I will instruct you and teach you in the way which you should go; I will counsel you with My eye upon you. Psalm 32:8

Do you believe God has His eye on you? Why or why not?

Call to Me and I will answer you, and I will tell you great and mighty things, which you do not know. Jeremiah 33:3

Specifically, what do you need to know?

I will make all My mountains a road, and My highways will be raised up. Isaiah 49:11.

Did you know that the word *highway* is in the Bible? Maybe you're living in some pretty tough circumstances right now and you need God to make a way — a highway right through the mountain that obstructs your path.

Where do you need God to make a way where there seems to be no way?

Make me know Your ways, O Lord; Teach me Your paths. Lead me in Your truth and teach me, for You are the God of my salvation; for You I wait all the day (Psalm 25:4–5).

Where and when will you go to spend time with God so He can teach you what to do?

Make plans, include God in your decisions, and seek His will. Then rest in peace with your fourth cup of tea.

Prayer

God, help me know

- what to do.
- what to say.
- what to think.
- where to go.

For Reflection

What did God reveal about His character?

How have you been challenged in a specific area of your life?

How will you apply the passage to your daily routine?

How is your faith being strengthened?

Ж

It doesn't make sense that our decisions would make much of a difference in the overall scheme of things, but regardless of the short time we have on earth, God will lead us to make decisions that have a shining, everlasting impact.

Ж

Godly Friends Chime In

SAVANNAH says, "Good Stuff! Hold your plans loosely, because God may change them. After bone cancer, bladder cancer, and heart failure three times, I know it's foolish to boast of tomorrow because He holds the plans. He kept me here for a reason and that purpose is for Him. Make each day count and be an influence. To sit with all this burning fire inside of me and not shout it out just feels bizarre to me! Currently, my ministry is in my home. It's crazy because my life before being a Jesus follower was the exact opposite. I was living for Me! Me! Me! I praise God for setting my feet on a rock and giving me a firm place to stand — Jesus! If He gives me tomorrow, I will boast of the Lord!"

GLORIA shares, "I was ready for a long-awaited happy occasion to travel to Texas for my niece's wedding. The airline tickets were purchased as well as my new outfit. I was expected to help with the decorating, food, and a lot of the last-minute planning. Suddenly, though, a world pandemic was announced, along with the governor issuing a stay at home order. COVID-19 was all over the news and in most everyone's conversations. My sister decided to stay home in Tennessee, but I decided that I was going anyway. *I'm needed and I can't let my niece down*, I reasoned. Then early one morning I was studying James Week 4, Day 4 of this study, when the prayer, *Help me know what to do, say, think, and go*, flew off the page. So I asked God what to do about my wedding trip and flight, what to say to my niece if I didn't go, and to help me think this through realistically and in obedience. Isaiah 30:21 tells us that we will hear from God which way to go. And I did! I sensed Him telling me to stay put. I immediately breathed a sigh of relief. The decision was made. My family understood my decision and sent me a video of the wedding. A later trip was planned. Better days are ahead and I'm so thankful that God really does know best."

Week 4, Day 5

Oblivious

Read James 4:17:

To one who knows the right thing to do and does not do it, to him it is sin.

Recall your favorite childhood Bible stories. Was your beloved story baby Moses in the basket? Noah's ark? David and Goliath? Maybe it was the story of Jonah. You know, the guy who got swallowed up by a whale.

I loved telling the story of Jonah to my children. He was an upright, godly man who didn't carouse with the wicked people — especially the wicked people of Nineveh. In the eyes of onlookers, Jonah was a true man of God. So, it's not what Jonah did that got him swallowed by a giant fish . . . it's what *he didn't do*. God told Jonah to go to Nineveh and tell the people to turn from their wicked ways and follow God. But Jonah didn't want to. He disobeyed God and instead bought a ticket and sailed away on a ship.

Jonah was guilty of the sin of omission. *Webster* defines omission as "something neglected or left undone."[66] This is different from a sin of commission — a willful sin that violates what God tells us not to do. The sin of omission is *not* doing what we should do. Neglecting to care for a family member is an example of the sin of omission.

What are some other common sins that we're possibly guilty of *not doing?*

What about prayer? How can a lack of prayer become a sin for a Christ-follower?

I can relate to Paul's frustration when he wrote this in Romans 7:15: *What I am doing, I do not understand; for I am not practicing what I would like to do, but I am doing the very thing I hate.*

In what ways can you relate to Paul's frustration?

Most of us feel like Paul. We don't want to disregard God's command but sometimes we're oblivious to what we're refusing to do. And it's just as exasperating when we don't feel like we're hearing God's voice. "How can I know what to do if He doesn't tell me?" you might wonder. Perhaps, though, we need to tune out the noisy distractions such as mental chaos and busyness and set aside time to be quiet and listen for God. God speaks in a variety of ways:

1. He speaks through His Holy Word. The stories are used to build our faith and to teach us how to apply biblical principles to our specific and personal situation. While engaged in Bible reading, we discover the character of God, learn His ways, and begin to see things from His perspective. Then our ears become attuned to His voice.

2. Often God will confirm what we believe God is speaking through other godly people, such as a pastor, counselor, or close friend.

3. God also speaks to our heart and mind and spirit when we're talking to Him through prayer.

Look at the following Scriptures and describe what God tells us to do … or not do.

1 John 3:17–18

John 14:15

1 Samuel 12:23

1 Thessalonians 5:17

Galatians 5:13

John 15:12

Ephesians 4:32

Which of the previous verses spoke to you personally? Is there another verse that God has placed on your heart? If so, which one?

Which of the following could be the motivation to commit a sin of omission? Circle all that apply.

Fear   Complacency   Pride

Self-reliance   Arrogance   Selfishness

Justification   Other _____

All of these could be reasons for us to reject what God tells us to do. But we can have joy because God will show us how to accomplish what He's asked us to do.

Recall Matthew 5:16 which tells us: ***Let your light shine before men in such a way that they may see your good works, and glorify your Father who is in heaven.*** What do you personally need to let go of so that you can shine?

How can passively ignoring the wrong that goes on around us be disobedience? What can Christians do to make a difference?

When we don't stand for what is right, our silence can lead to a sin of omission. That is what happened to Jonah. God told him what to do and Jonah resisted. But God pursued him with discipline until Jonah confessed his sin and surrendered to God's will. The people of Nineveh listened to Jonah's rebuke, and, believing in God, confessed their sins to Him.

Luke 11:28 tells us: *Blessed are those who hear the word of God and observe it.*

And Deuteronomy 28:1–2 we read: *Now it shall be, if you diligently obey the Lord your God, being careful to do all His commandments which I command you today, the Lord your God will set you high above all the nations of the earth. "All these blessings will come upon you and overtake you if you obey the Lord your God.*

According to these verses, what part is your responsibility? What steps will you take to be obedient?

Jonah eventually took action and accomplished what God told him to do. You, too, can depend on God's strength to enable you to do what God asks of you.

Notes

Prayer

God, help me know

- what to do.
- what to say.
- what to think.
- where to go.

For Reflection

What did God reveal about His character?

How have you been challenged in a specific area of your life?

How will you apply the passage to your daily routine?

How is your faith being strengthened?

X

It doesn't make sense to reject what's justified or considered a normal reaction by our culture and do what's right in the eyes of God instead, but when we're obedient, blessings such as joy, peace and freedom abound.

X

Godly Friends Chime In

SAVANNAH says, "I love a good accountability partner — someone who holds me accountable for my conversation and my conduct. It's difficult for me, however, to hold the ones we truly love accountable without feeling like I'm judging them. But I'm learning to pray for them and asking God to show me through His Word the truth to share."

DEBBIE adds, " I've learned to be more intentional about listening for God's voice, and sometimes we listen with my eyes. While watching a beautiful sunrise, God says that His mercy and kindness is new that morning. While watching the mama bird feed her babies in the nest she built in the birdhouse on my front porch, God says that He takes care of the birds and He'll take care of me, too. While sitting on the beach watching the tides roll in and roll out, God shows His faithfulness. Yes, God is speaking . . . sometimes we just need to open our eyes and look around."

Truths from James 4

- Depend on God for all your needs.
- Ask God for help with everything.
- God will help you make wise decisions.
- Seek God's will.
- Boasting is arrogance.
- It is a sin to disobey God.
- Surrender to the Holy Spirit.
- Those who are humble will be exalted.
- Friendship with the world is opposition to God.
- Confess your sins and draw near to God.
- Unfaithfulness to God is spiritual adultery.
- Conforming to the world's standards makes us an enemy of Christ.
- Submit to God and resist the devil.
- God is the ultimate judge.
- Consult with God about your plans, hopes, and dreams.
- Life is brief; make the most of every day.
- Walk with God by spending time in His Word.
- Maintain steadfast devotion.
- Wait in hopeful expectation.
- Resist idols and be devoted to God.
- God is jealous for you.
- Approach God in humility.
- Refrain from criticism.
- Biblical correction is motivated by love.
- Confrontation requires prayer.
- Accountability among friends is built on a trusting relationship.
- A sin of omission is not doing what we know we should.
- A sin of commission violates God's law.

Week 5, Day 1

Everlasting Treasures

Read James 5:1–6

> *Come now, you rich, weep and howl for your miseries which are coming upon you. Your riches have rotted and your garments have become moth-eaten. Your gold and your silver have rusted; and their rust will be a witness against you and will consume your flesh like fire. It is in the last days that you have stored up your treasure! Behold, the pay of the laborers who mowed your fields, and which has been withheld by you, cries out against you; and the outcry of those who did the harvesting has reached the ears of the Lord of Sabaoth. You have lived luxuriously on the earth and led a life of wanton pleasure; you have fattened your hearts in a day of slaughter. You have condemned and, put to death the righteous man; he does not resist you.*

*H*ave you seen the television reality show *Gold Rush* that airs on the Discovery Channel? The series follows miners in Alaska searching for gold — a shiny treasure that will, hopefully, change their lives. The show is meant to be entertaining, and perhaps spark in us a dream about what we'd do with revenue from a gold discovery.

Most of us aren't on an expedition to find gold. But what treasures are we pursuing? To answer that question, we first have to know what *treasure* means. *Merriam-Webster* provides two definitions:

- Wealth (such as money, jewels, or precious metals) stored up or hoarded; buried treasure; wealth of any kind or in any form; riches; a store of money in reserve.

- Something of great worth or value; a person esteemed as rare or precious; a collection of precious things.[67]

Notes   In this last chapter of James, James speaks to rich people again and links their abuse of power, unfair treatment, and immoral behavior, as the reason they became wealthy. What they will ultimately achieve, however, is misery. Do you see any resemblance between the behaviors of first-century Christians and those of twenty-first century Christians? If so, what are those similarities?

James didn't call all rich people *ungodly*; he called out their behaviors as ungodly. What were the rich doing? Specifically, how were they treating their employees?

What other ungodly behaviors can you identify in this passage?

The unfair treatment of employees, selfish behaviors, and elevated self-worth, preceded a luxurious lifestyle.

How can striving for and obtaining wealth lead to:

An inflated opinion of oneself?

Self-sufficiency?

Abuse of power?

Attempts to influence authority?

Bribery or blackmail?

In addition to those behaviors listed in James five, what other behaviors might an ungodly person seeking earthly riches and pleasures exhibit? Circle all that apply:

Covetousness	Generosity	Hoarding	Oppression/Cruelty
Politeness	Injustice	Humility	Cordiality
Debauchery	Immorality	Restraint	Pride
Willingness	Fairness	Disrespect	Unkindness
Selfishness	Arrogance	Love	Selflessness

Look at the behaviors you didn't circle. Those are the actions and attitudes of a godly person, with or without wealth. What is the difference between the rich who are ungodly and the wealthy who are righteous?

James' words are becoming less about the size of our pocketbook and more about what we're in pursuit of, what we'll do to achieve these goals, and what we truly treasure.

Our treasure is what we strive for . . . how we achieve it . . . what we'll sacrifice . . . and how we use what we're blessed with. Our behaviors reflect what we treasure and consider precious.

If you're not wealthy, pretend you are. And if you're rich, think about your finances. Now answer this question: What will you do with your abundance of money?

Most of us would say that we'd share with our family. We'd also want to help the impoverished and attempt to make a difference in our communities. And that's the point. Even if we're not rich, we're generous with what we have because God tells us to be. And we're fair, because God loves justice.

Matthew 6:19–21 tells us: *Do not store up for yourselves treasures on earth, where moth and rust destroy, and where thieves break in and steal. But store up for yourselves treasures in heaven, where neither moth nor rust destroys, and where thieves do not break in or steal; for where your treasure is, there your heart will be also.*

What do you treasure?

In what ways are you seeking *that* treasure?

What would those closest to you say you treasure?

When we begin to treasure Jesus Christ, our view of money changes. Think about the material possessions God has given you. In what ways can you use them for God's glory — to honor him and point others to him?

Read Proverbs 2:1–9: *My son, if you will receive my words and treasure my commandments within you, make your ear attentive to wisdom, incline your heart to understanding; for if you cry for discernment, lift your voice for understanding; if you seek her as silver and search for her as for hidden treasures; then you will discern the fear of the LORD and discover the knowledge of God. For the LORD gives wisdom; from His mouth come knowledge and understanding. He stores up sound wisdom for the upright; He is a shield to those who walk in integrity, guarding the paths of justice, and He preserves the way of His godly ones. Then you will discern righteousness and justice and equity and every good course.*

Based on this passage, what does God want us to treasure?

Recently, God gave me a new perspective on 1 Corinthians 3:9–15. Read the passage here:

We are God's fellow workers; you are God's field, God's building. According to the grace of God which was given to me, like a wise master builder I laid a foundation, and another is building on it. But each man must be careful how he builds on it. For no man can lay a foundation other than the one which is laid, which is Jesus Christ. Now if any man builds on the foundation with gold, silver, precious stones, wood, hay, straw, each man's work will become evident; for the day will show it because it is to be revealed with fire, and the fire itself will test the quality of each man's work. If any man's work which he has built on it remains, he will receive a reward. If any man's work is burned up, he will suffer loss; but he himself will be saved, yet so as through fire.

God prepared me decades ago to direct Shine Camp — a day camp for teen girls in my town. God has given me everything I need to operate the camp, including a talented team. I've invested financially in this camp, but I've never made a personal profit. The same is true with my published books. The camp and my books teach, inspire, and encourage women to live by godly principles. After reading the above passage, I realized that both the camp and my books are spiritual gold. I cannot give them a monetary value. But they are precious jewels to the women whose lives have been changed by them.

What we treasure is important to God.

What else does God treasure? Us.

Deuteronomy 7:6 tells us: *You are a holy people to the Lord your God; the Lord your God has chosen you to be a people for Himself, a special treasure above all the peoples on the face of the earth* (NKJV).

Meditate on that fantastic truth. It's almost incomprehensible. But we're God's treasured possession!

Is He ours? Do we treasure Jesus Christ? When Jesus is our treasure, we'll:

- Hold Him close in our hearts and meet with Him in Bible reading and prayer.
- Protect and defend His name, not misuse it, or laugh when others do.
- Tell others about our great love for Him.
- Use our monetary riches to spread the gospel.

The godly, the ungodly; the wealthy, the poor; the arrogant, the humble. We all have one thing in common — we'll all eventually die. And what we treasured on earth will be left to decay and disappear. But, at death, our everlasting treasures will be revealed.

God has all the riches in the world, yet He seeks us, loves us, and makes us His special treasure. Let's begin our expedition today and seek after everlasting treasures.

Prayer

God, help me know

- what to do.
- what to say.
- what to think.
- where to go.

For Reflection

What did God reveal about His character?

How have you been challenged in a specific area of your life?

How will you apply the passage to your daily routine?

How is your faith being strengthened?

X

It doesn't make sense to run from what the world pursues, but because we're God's special treasure, we use the possessions He gives us for His glory and make Him our special treasure too.

X

Godly Friends Chime In

TAMRA speaks up: "I've personally experienced that the closer I draw to the heart of God, my view of treasure changes, too."

SAVANNAH agrees. "Before I fully gave my heart over to Jesus, I wanted everything — and didn't think twice about the debt it would bring. But now, I've discovered that my desires truly have changed because I'm in hot pursuit of Jesus. There's a distinct difference in the godly rich person who is also in pursuit of Jesus. It's not hard to notice. Remember, we are just managers of whatever God gives us."

Week 5, Day 2

Patience

Read James 5:7–11:

Be patient, brethren, until the coming of the Lord. The farmer waits for the precious produce of the soil, being patient about it, until it gets the early and late rains. You too be patient; strengthen your hearts, for the coming of the Lord is near. Do not complain, brethren, against one another, so that you yourselves may not be judged; behold, the Judge is standing right at the door. As an example, brethren, of suffering and patience, take the prophets who spoke in the name of the Lord. We count those blessed who endured. You have heard of the endurance of Job and have seen the outcome of the Lord's dealings, that the Lord is full of compassion and is merciful.

On a scale of 1–10, with 10 being the most, how patient do you consider yourself to be?

1   2   3   4   5   6   7   8   9   10

Does your level of patience depend on the situation? If yes, explain. If no, why not?

I asked my husband the same questions using the same scale, but referring to two scenarios. I asked, "How patient do you feel you are when you're stuck behind a slow driver?"

Looking rather embarrassed, he honestly replied, "Somewhere between two and three."

Then I asked, "How patient are you while waiting to be cancer free?

With radiant hope he responded, "An eight or a nine."

What about you? Do you have more patience when there's more at stake? Why or why not?

We all have opportunities to wait. If you're like me, sometimes you're patient and sometimes you're not.

- We wait to be cured of illness.
- We wait for the country to return to normal after a pandemic.
- We wait for weddings and for babies to be born.
- We wait for prodigals to come home.
- We wait for a start date on a new job and for retirement.
- We wait for loved ones to accept Jesus as Savior.

And patience, or a need for patience, is our companion on the journey.

Merriam-Webster defines *patience* as "the ability to wait for a long time without becoming annoyed or upset." [68] *To wait* as used in the original Hebrew, means to hope, look eagerly for, expect.[69]

What specifically are you waiting for — something to happen or something to end?

Why do you think God asks us to wait?

Mary and Martha waited for Jesus to come heal their brother, Lazarus. But by the time Jesus arrived, Lazarus had died. Read John 11:1–45. Mary, Martha, and Lazarus were close friends with Jesus.

When Lazarus became sick, the sisters sent a message to Jesus.

What did the message say? (John 11:3)

Jesus didn't go for two more days, and by that time Lazarus had died. How do you think the sisters felt at that point?

When Martha finally saw Jesus, she said something very significant. What was it? (John 11:21)

What do you think Martha's tone was?

"If you had been here" reveals an attitude of belief in Jesus and His capabilities. But it also indicates a shift in emotions: blame and unmet expectation. Martha expected Jesus to come, and because He didn't, Lazarus died. She couldn't see past her disappointment — which is normal in the first few raw days of grief — to understand that Jesus had a purpose in His delay. But God is patient with us as we journey through grief.

How did Jesus respond?

How did the miracle affect the people watching? (John 11:45)

In what way do you think Martha was changed?

Later, Martha saw the greater miracle — that many believed. God has a purpose when He asks us to wait.

You may recall from Week 1, Day 5 of this study, that patience is a fruit of the Spirit — evidence of a Spirit-filled life. The synonym *longsuffering* is used in the NKJV and KJV; *forbearance* is used in the NIV.

When I first began studying the fruit of the Spirit decades ago, I was eager to demonstrate each of the fruit as evidence that my faith was real. I set out on a mission to demonstrate each fruit by the end of the week! That was a mistake, and I laugh about it now.

My heart was right — I was genuinely motivated by my love for Christ. But after a few days of failing miserably, I became discouraged and frustrated. My mistake was forcing these behaviors — whether they were real or not. I could fake *patience* with a smile, but my insides were screaming!

But God tenderly taught me that developing the fruit of the Spirit requires time. I should have been focused on God Himself by getting into God's Word, learning to depend on Him during difficult trials, developing a relationship with God through prayer, and obeying His commandments.

When we focus on developing our relationship with God, the fruit of the Spirit begins to grow within us. We won't have to strive — fruit emerges naturally as we become closer to Christ. Ironically, to produce patience, I had to wait for the Lord to prune and refine me.

What is the most difficult part for you personally when waiting for a prayer to be answered?

In what ways have you in the past, or are you now, exhibiting endurance through a tough situation?

James uses farming, the suffering of the Old Testament prophets, and the example of Job to explain endurance and patience.

1. Farmers wait with expectation.

   The farmer plants the seed, then waits to reap the harvest. The farmer stays busy while waiting. He will have storms to deal with or other disruptions. Like the farmer, we wait for the seeds we've planted — prayers or anything we've hoped or planned for — to come to fruition. And we, too, should stay busy.

   In what ways are you being disrupted today?

   Keep your eyes focused on the symbolic harvest — that which is sure to come. Hebrews 10:36 tells us: *You need to persevere so that when you have done the will of God, you will receive what he has promised.*

2. The prophets of the Old Testament suffered.

   The people's choices affected the prophets, yet God continued to care for the people. Sometimes we suffer for the sake of Christ during a waiting period. Remember Elijah whom we discussed in James 4? The people of Israel went for three years without rain as discipline for their rebellion. Elijah patiently suffered with them, for the sake of Christ.

   Read Matthew 5:10–12. When, if ever, have you suffered for the sake of Christ?

How can any tragedy, for example, the pandemic of 2020, be a time of suffering for the sake of Christ?

3. Job patiently endured hardship.

When someone shows endurance through trials and perseverance in hardship, we say that person has the "patience of Job." Read Job 1:1–22. How is Job described? (v. 1)

What did he own? (vv. 2–3)

What did he lose? (vv. 6–19)

How did Job respond to his suffering? (vv. 21–22)

Whom did Job refuse to blame? (v.22)

Read Job 2:10. What was Job's response to his wife?

Chapters 3–42 contain conversations between Job and his friends, and Job and God. Most of the time, when Job asked the tough questions of God, he didn't get an answer. What he did get was better, though. He got God. And before everything was restored, he was satisfied with being in the presence of the Lord. When we consider this situation in its entirety — from Job's test, his response, and outcome, how was it possible for Job to survive such tragedy?

Waiting is especially difficult during a season of hardship, but adversity is also an opportunity to

- exercise our faith muscles.
- develop a more intimate relationship with Jesus Christ.
- trust God more.
- relinquish control.
- discern the will of God.

Becoming patient is achievable. Like anything else we desire, from material needs to wisdom, we pray and ask God to help us obtain it. Patience is no exception. We begin by recognizing our need and admitting our shortcomings. Then we ask God to help us in that area. We read our Bible and pray specifically about becoming a person who trusts God's timing for long-awaited events. We can pray for patience while driving or waiting in line.

As you wait, you can:

- Cultivate an attitude of gratitude. Thank God for His blessings in your life.
- Cry out to God — with words, moans, screams, or tears. Choose to believe He will hear and answer. It's mind over matter. Don't trust your up-and-down feelings; trust God's Word.
- Anticipate and expect God to bring about a good result. Recall Romans 8:28 which tells us that *God causes all things to work together for good to those who love God, to those who are called according to His purpose.*

- Meditate on God's promises. Psalm 27:14 tells us to *wait for the Lord; be strong and let your heart take courage; yes, wait for the Lord.* Lamentations 3:25 tells us *the Lord is good to those who wait for Him, to the person who seeks Him.* Isaiah 40:31 tells us *those who wait for the Lord will gain new strength; they will mount up with wings like eagles, they will run and not get tired, they will walk and not become weary.*

- Trust that God's timing is perfect. God is not in a hurry to produce a perfect result.

- Praise God for His work in the past. Tell others about the good things He has done. Remembering God's faithfulness in the past will encourage you.

- Do not fret. Read King David's words in Psalm 37:1–8: *Do not fret because of evildoers, be not envious toward wrongdoers. For they will wither quickly like the grass and fade like the green herb. Trust in the LORD and do good; Dwell in the land and cultivate faithfulness. Delight yourself in the Lord; and He will give you the desires of your heart. Commit your way to the LORD, trust also in Him, and He will do it. He will bring forth your righteousness as the light and your judgment as the noonday. Rest in the LORD and wait patiently for Him; Do not fret because of him who prospers in his way, because of the man who carries out wicked schemes. Cease from anger and forsake wrath; do not fret; it leads only to evildoing.*

How many times did David tell us not to fret?

What are we told to do while waiting patiently for God to act?

What are we to cultivate?

How would you summarize and teach this passage to a child?

Author and Bible teacher Charles Stanley wrote, "You can trust that if He [God] asks you to wait, He has something more wonderful in mind than you could ever provide for yourself."[70]

Ironically, we wait to become patient, too.

Prayer

God, help me know

- what to do.
- what to say.
- what to think.
- where to go.

It doesn't make sense that we can wait patiently, especially in times of adversity, but patience because possible when we spend time in God's Word and learn to trust His timing.

)(

For Reflection

What did God reveal about His character?

How have you been challenged in a specific area of your life?

How will you apply the passage to your daily routine?

How is your faith being strengthened?

Godly Friends Chime In

CAROL says, "I love this. Being older and looking back over the years, I give thanks to the Lord for the circumstances that He has allowed to give me confidence that He is in charge. My timing is only as good as He makes it be. And He has proved over and over that all things work for good to those who love the Lord."

SAVANNAH responds, "Apart from Jesus, I have zero patience! Patience becomes supernatural at this point — God changing me. Proverbs 3:5–6 is my sidekick. Trust, Savannah, trust Him! I keep this cheerleader talk on repeat. Today, I am specifically waiting for God to restore our nation. I'm waiting on God's movement — not man's. I'm also waiting for God to remove impurities from my heart. God is in control and He's always up to something good!"

I Swear (Not)!

Read James 5:12:

> *Above all, my brethren, do not swear, either by heaven or by earth or with any other oath; but your yes is to be yes, and your no, no, so that you may not fall under judgment.*

*B*ased on the title, you may have thought this study was about cursing. And it could be, since the word *swear* could mean either to curse or take an oath. Today's passage is about taking oaths.

Based on your personal experience, do you define *swearing* as cursing or as taking an oath? When, if ever, have you used the word *swear*? Was it in casual conversation or in a court of law?

My first recollection of hearing the word *swear* was on the playground at school with my third-grade classmates trading Barbie doll clothes. Inevitably someone would forget to bring their doll clothes to exchange but still wanted to take part in the trade. She'd say, "I swear I'll bring them tomorrow." Then someone else would respond, "You're not supposed to swear!" I, too, had learned that as a Christian, no swearing was allowed. But I didn't know why.

An oath is a solemn promise to tell the absolute truth. It could be made as a vow in court, or in front of a witness. "That's why it's odd that an oath can also be an angry outburst of obscene words."[71]

In the Old Testament, God used oaths to show He would do what He promised. James warned, then, that we should not take an oath in casual conversation, because that would be disrespectful to God.[72]

Undoubtedly, you've heard someone swear on someone's life. For example, "I swear on my mother's life." What do you think that means?

Many explanations exist, but a majority of people seem to think that if you swear by someone's name, you're suggesting that person would verify that you're telling the truth.

In the context of James 5:12, Matthew Henry wrote, "All customary needless swearing is all along in scripture condemned, as a very grievous sin. . . . The Jews thought if they did but omit the great oath . . . they were safe. But they grew so profane as to swear by the creature, as if it were God. . . . Stand on your word, and be true to it, so as to give no occasion for your being suspected of falsehood. It is being suspected of falsehood that leads men to swearing."[73]

What do you think? Is your word enough to stand on?

Piper says, "The assumption is that you come into this courtroom or some situation and you are not really committed to tell the truth, so maybe we could up your commitment to tell the truth if we could get you to associate your telling of the truth or your lying with the desecration of some sacred object like your mother's name or dad's grave or the name of God or the Bible."[74]

Wow. We're either desperate for the truth or to prove that we're telling the truth.

At first glance, James 5:12 seems out of place or random. The previous verses were about patience and Job's suffering. But during suffering we may say things we don't mean, including making promises or bargaining with God, even swearing to God.

Instead of swearing, James says to show Christian integrity and respond with a truthful _____ or _____ (James 5:12).

Read Matthew 5:33–37 written here:

Again, you have heard that the ancients were told, 'YOU SHALL NOT MAKE FALSE VOWS, BUT SHALL FULFILL YOUR VOWS TO THE LORD.' But I say to you, make no oath at all, either by heaven, for it is the throne of God, or by the earth, for it is the footstool of His feet, or by Jerusalem, for it is the city of the Great King. Nor shall you make an oath by your head, for you cannot make one hair white or black. But let your statement be, 'Yes, yes' or 'No, no'; anything beyond these is of evil.

How will you apply this biblical truth in your life?

Swearing is a tough subject because well-established, thoughtful commentators approach the topic from different perspectives:

- Matthew Henry calls swearing a sin.

- Wiersbe says there's no indication that swearing in a court of law would be a sin, although we shouldn't do it.

- Piper explains what he would do if asked to swear on a Bible in court. He says, "Your honor, my commitment to the truth and to the Lord of the truth, Jesus Christ, leads me to believe that it would dishonor both my commitment to the Lord and the Lord himself if I needed to put my hand on this sacred book to guarantee my truthfulness. I am totally committed to the truth and to the Lord of the truth. So I ask that I be permitted to act without such an oath, but I do promise in reliance on the help of the Lord Jesus to tell the truth, the whole truth, and nothing but the truth."[75]

As we navigate our way through this life, the best thing to do is draw near to God, read His Word and pray, and then allow His Holy Spirit to tell us what to do. But we can agree on one thing: We should be people with a reputation for keeping our word, and we should be known for telling the truth.

Prayer

God, help me know

- what to do.
- what to say.
- what to think.
- where to go.

For Reflection

What did God reveal about His character?

How have you been challenged in a specific area of your life?

How will you apply the passage to your daily routine?

How is your faith being strengthened?

Ж

It doesn't make sense that our reputation as a trustworthy person can be established with a simple yes or no, but because our reputation precedes us, we're known to be trustworthy.

Ж

Godly Friends Chime In

SAVANNAH says, "I think it's insecurity that's behind why people swear. We care so much about what other people think of us, that we have something to prove. Having a clear conscience is important to me . . . so I will simply let my 'yes' and my 'no' be enough."

CAROL adds, "Many years ago I heard an excellent message on this. I came away with a strong reverence for the Lord and swearing an oath to God. What the Lord says, He means, and we can be confident that He is accountable. Swearing unto the Lord is not to be taken lightly just as 'I promise' rolls off of some people's tongues too easily. Because we are Christians, what we say reflects not only on us, but also on the Lord. No matter how good our intentions are, circumstances, or negligence may prevent us from keeping an oath or promise. It is better not to put ourselves in that position. I have tried to teach my children to say 'I will do my best.'"

Week 5, Day 4

All Kinds of Sickness

Read James 5:13–15:

Is anyone among you suffering? Then he must pray. Is anyone cheerful? He is to sing praises. Is anyone among you sick? Then he must call for the elders of the church and they are to pray over him, anointing him with oil in the name of the Lord; and the prayer offered in faith will restore the one who is sick, and the Lord will raise him up, and if he has committed sins, they will be forgiven him.

*E*veryone has been affected by sickness at one time or another. There are four main types:

- disease or physical illnesses
- mental sickness, as in an unsound mind
- emotional illness, such as depression
- spiritual or misguided moral sickness, such as believing wrong is acceptable [76]

Are you more familiar with some types of illness than others? If so, which ones?

We all desire good health for ourselves and our loved ones. In a perfect world, there would be no disease, illness, death, paralysis, despair, dementia, depression, or any other ailment. But our world is broken; as a result, people are afflicted with a broad range of sicknesses.

James is ambiguous about the specific sickness and healing to which he refers. But he may have been vague intentionally. The term translated as "sick" comes from the Greek word *asthenei*, which refers to all kinds of sickness. [77]

Notes   An article on chronic diseases in the United States reported that approximately 45 percent, or 133 million, of all Americans suffer from various chronic diseases — including cancer, diabetes, hypertension, stroke, heart disease, respiratory diseases, arthritis, and obesity.[78]

And that's just physical sickness. According to an article in the 2017 National Institute of Mental Health, approximately 46.6 million adults in the United States aged 18 or older live with a mental illness. That's one in five adults, or 18.9 percent of the population.[79]

And yes, the American Heart Association reports that a broken heart is real. In fact, it has a name: stress-induced cardiomyopathy or takotsubo cardiomyopathy.[80]

In many instances, illnesses can be treated with a prescribed drug to help the person function better.

Information on the number of those affected with spiritual sickness is not as readily available. Yet, all around us is evidence of spiritual deprivation. And unlike other illnesses, there isn't a curative drug or diet — at least not a physical one.

In Bible time, Jews applied oil to sores and wounds; they also used it for other medicinal purposes. The use of oil was part of the healing process. The word *oil* in today's verses is the Greek word *elaio,* which refers to olive oil.[81] Anointing means *smearing* or *rubbing* with oil. James isn't referring to the healing abilities of these oils; he's saying that the prayer associated with these practices brings healing.

For unbelievers, spiritual sickness is a death sentence. Ephesians 2:1 tells us: **You were dead in your trespasses and sins.** Believers can also be spiritually sick. Unconfessed sin and failure to grow spiritually cause a believer to deteriorate and decline.

Read Matthew 9:9–13.

Whom did Jesus invite to a meal? (v. 9)

What kind of people ate with Jesus and His disciples on this occasion? (v. 10)

What question did the Pharisees ask the disciples? (v. 11)

Overhearing their question, Jesus answered. What did He say to them? (v. 12)

Jesus identified Himself as a physician. In what way were these people sick?

Many Bible scholars agree that Psalm 6 is one of the penitential psalms King David wrote after his sin with Bathsheba. His downfall began with sin, which left him spiritually sick for approximately one year. But spiritual sickness can be connected to emotional, mental, and physical sickness.

Read Psalm 6:2–7. How did David describe his physical body?

What words indicate his depressed state? (vv. 2–3, 6–7)

David wrote again about the consequences of his sin in Psalm 32:3. What happened to David's body?

Hiding his sin brought emotional distress. How did he describe his level of strength? (v. 4)

Sickness touched every area of David's life — not just his physical and his mental state. His shame and guilt stood as a wall between himself and God. David's emotions and his social interactions with others were affected. But then something happened. David finally confessed his sin. How did God respond? (v. 5)

Are you, like David, sick with the weight of unconfessed sin?

Read Psalm 32:11. After confession and forgiveness, David's emotional state changed. What emotion did he experience? What advice did he give?

In this instance, sin was the cause of David's misery.

As already mentioned, drugs or diet can be a successful method of treatment for various sicknesses. If we're vomiting, for example, we may try and determine what we ate and then take nausea medicine.

With spiritual sickness, we also have to look at our spiritual diet and consider what we're feeding on. If we've neglected spiritual food, we'll become spiritually malnourished.

How did Jeremiah stay spiritually healthy? His spiritual diet is identified in Jeremiah 15:16. He wrote: *Your words [God] were found and I ate them, and Your words became for me a joy and the delight of my heart.*

He treasured God's words more than food. Do we? More specifically, do *you* treasure God's Holy Word? If yes, how do you demonstrate that? If no, can you identify why not?

God's Word does for the soul what food does for the human body; it permits us to be spiritually vital and it transforms our heart and soul. We need the Bible to

- dispel the poisonous, toxic lies of Satan and quench our thirst for truth.
- help us move forward and grow.
- make us strong and courageous.
- energize our spirit.
- cushion us against the enemies' attacks.

Some people only reach for the Bible when their world falls apart, just as some people only take vitamins when their body needs to replenish them. But for us to stay spiritually nourished, we need to follow Jeremiah's example. Jeremiah feasted on God's Word the way we consume food. Psalm 34:8 tells us: *O taste and see that the Lord is good; how blessed is the man who takes refuge in Him!* In this context, taste doesn't imply a nibble. Taste means to feed on the Word of God.

Which of these statements best describes you?

- ❑ I nibble on God's Word occasionally.
- ❑ I feed on God's Word regularly.

If you chose nibble, what is the most difficult part about reading the Bible?

If you chose feed, what motivates you to read your Bible regularly?

In Scripture, when someone was sick, loved ones called for a healer or elder of the church. Today we are encouraged to contact our church, a Sunday school class, a connect or life group member, or mentor. Whom do you call when you're sick?

Many healings and miracles are recorded in the Bible for our encouragement. But God didn't heal every person, and neither is every person healed today. Paul was not healed of his thorn (2 Corinthians 12:8). God has a purpose for those He does not heal, and with that purpose He provides grace and strength.

Reread James 5:15. What do you think it means to pray in faith?

Some consider Matthew 26:42 to be the greatest example of faith. Jesus was in Gethsemane the night before He was crucified. He prayed, *"My Father, if this cannot pass away unless I drink it, Your will be done."* Having faith doesn't mean you're going to get your way; rather having faith in God is believing in His character, His plans and purpose, and accepting that God gets His way — even in sickness and death.

Psalm 147:3 tells us, *He heals the brokenhearted and binds up their wounds.* The word translated *heal* is the Hebrew word *rapha* which means to repair and thoroughly make whole; to mend by stitching. The word *broken* in the Hebrew is *shabar* and means to break into pieces. Broken-hearted in this context means crushed or destroyed or torn.[82]

Do you feel shattered emotionally? Are you exhausted from the pain of your fragmented pieces?

The Great Physician heals our hurts by stitching us back together. Referring again to Psalm 147:3, the Hebrew word for *bind up* is *chabash*; it means to wrap up our wounds or hurts.[83] Picture God wrapping a bandage around your pain. How does it make you feel?

We shouldn't be surprised that James writes about singing songs and being joyful in the same context as sickness. Praise and worship music can spark joy and be the perfect prescription for emotional/spiritual health. Proverbs 17:22 tells us *a joyful heart is good medicine, but a broken spirit dries up the bones.*

No matter what area of sickness you're grappling with on your current journey, pray for healing. Pray in faith. Pray that God's will be done.

Notes

Prayer

God, help me know

- what to do.
- what to say.
- what to think.
- where to go.

For Reflection

What did God reveal about His character?

How have you been challenged in a specific area of your life?

How will you apply the passage to your daily routine?

How is your faith being strengthened?

Godly Friends Chime In

SAVANNAH agrees. "Yup! I've definitely felt the exact same way as David did in Psalm 6. There were times in my life when my conscience was not clean. It ate me alive. I have been morally sick, perhaps even dead in these times. But Jesus came and did for me what He did for Matthew, the tax collector. Thank You, Jesus! Our Spiritual diet matters! Pray in faith for healing, and pray God's will be done!" God literally healed me physically too. I'm addicted to God's Word!"

CINDY says, "Years ago I suffered from an illness in which my whole system was thrown off. I went to the doctor and was prescribed different medicines. I suffered for two years, having flair ups about every month or two. I went on a very restrictive diet to try to get my system back to normal, all to no avail. One night I was feeling particularly bad, as this illness was not just affecting me physically but also emotionally. In desperation I began praying to God asking Him to heal me of this illness. As I prayed, I felt something in my body change. I knew that I was healed. It's been over ten years and I have never had an issue with that illness again."

To be spiritually healthy, feed yourself with God's words. They:

Refresh the soul
The law of the Lord is perfect, restoring the soul; the testimony of the Lord is sure, making wise the simple. Psalm 19:7

Are better than gold
They are more precious than gold, than much pure gold. Psalm 19:10 (NIV)

Are sweet
How sweet are Your words to my taste! Yes, sweeter than honey to my mouth! Psalm 119:103

Make us wise
Heed instruction and be wise, and do not neglect it. Proverbs 8:22

Bring blessing
Blessed are those who hear the word of God and observe it. Luke 11:28

Are true
You are near, O Lord, and all Your commandments are truth. Psalm 119:151

Are perfect
As for God, His way is perfect: The Lord's word is flawless; He shields all who take refuge in Him. Psalm 18:30 (NIV)

Remain forever
The grass withers, the flower fades, but the word of our God stands forever. Isaiah 40:8

Give understanding
For the Lord gives wisdom; from His mouth come knowledge and understanding. Proverbs 2:6

Lead to successful living
COMMIT YOUR WORKS TO THE LORD AND YOUR PLANS WILL BE ESTABLISHED. PROVERBS 16:3

Are medicine
They are life to those who find them and health to all their body. Proverbs 4:22

Week 5, Day 5

Let's Pray

Read James 5:16–20:

Confess your sins to one another, and pray for one another so that you may be healed. The effective prayer of a righteous man can accomplish much. Elijah was a man with a nature like ours, and he prayed earnestly that it would not rain, and it did not rain on the earth for three years and six months. Then he prayed again, and the sky poured rain and the earth produced its fruit. My brethren, if any among you strays from the truth and one turns him back, let him know that he who turns a sinner from the error of his way will save his soul from death and will cover a multitude of sins.

I first learned about prayer when I was nine years old. I didn't know much about theology or special words that made a prayer more effective. But as a new believer, I realized I should pray. I understood that prayer was talking to God. So, I talked. Walking home from school, I asked God to keep the dogs away from me. I requested that God help me with my schoolwork too. I said simply, "Help me." I never questioned *if He could*. I always *knew He would*.

As I matured spiritually, I learned theological terms and heard others pray impressive prayers using fancy words. For a time, I mimicked those prayers. However, God led me back to my simple yet powerful childhood way of praying — powerful, because I prayed with humility. You'll recognize this prayer. We've prayed it since day one of our journey together:

God, *help me* know

- what to do.
- what to say.
- what to think.
- where to go.

This prayer invites God into every area of our lives.

Reread James 5:16. Compare it to the different translations, then circle the similar words in each.

The effectual fervent prayer of a righteous man availeth much. NKJV, KJV

The prayer of a righteous person is powerful and effective. NIV, CSB

The earnest prayer of a righteous person has great power and produces wonderful results. NLT

The prayer of a righteous person has great power as it is working. ESV

The prayer of a person living right with God is something powerful to be reckoned with. MSG

How would you explain this verse to a child?

Fervent can be defined as having great intensity of feelings, *effectual*, as effective and able to produce an effect, and *righteous* as acting in accord with divine or moral law.[84]

What are you passionately praying to God about at this stage in your journey?

In our passage today, James specifically named Elijah as a righteous man whose prayers saved a nation. Let's take a look at the event to which James was referring.

The people of Israel had corrupted themselves with pagan worship — the worship of idols. Elijah, whose name means, "Yahweh is my God," practiced monotheism and remained faithful to God. God had rescued His people from their bondage in Egypt, but they became distracted with earthly pleasures and appeared to forget His goodness. Elijah prayed that God would discipline and deliver

His people from spiritual adultery so they wouldn't be lost forever. Motivated from love, God disciplined His people and withheld rain for three and a half years (1 Kings 17–19). God's plan was not to kill off His people but to bring them back to Him. The discipline was manifested as drought and famine. Elijah witnessed his fellow Israelites' immense pain and hardship as they were disciplined for their disobedience and idol worship. Then Elijah went to the mountain and earnestly prayed seven times for rain. Fire came down, the rain poured, and the people were saved saved.

Have you experienced a drought in your personal life — a "drought" when God withheld His blessing?

In what ways do the Israelites forgetting about God's goodness compare to when we as Christians forget God's goodness?

In 2020, the world experienced a COVID-19 outbreak and a worldwide pandemic ensued. In what ways does the pandemic resemble the drought and famine recorded in First Kings?

How does the end of the drought and famine in Elijah's time bring you hope for today?

Prayer is a powerful weapon that draws us into God's plan and makes us a partner with Him. The following are suggestions for effective communication with God:

Pray Naturally

Use your own vocabulary and express yourself at your comfort level. You know better than anybody how to convey your feelings to God. Resist comparing your prayers to others. Just be you. Jeremiah 29:12 says: *Then you will call upon Me and come and pray to Me, and I will listen to you.*

Be Real

Your heart is your true self. As best you can, talk to God in an open, honest way about the yucky stuff that's hiding deep within your heart and that you normally wouldn't admit to others, to God, and maybe even to yourself. Tell God what's really on your mind. Sometimes we have to start with some questions or opinions: His timing stinks, or He doesn't appear to care, or you doubt His goodness and you're disappointed. God created you and knows your emotional state of mind, your flaws, and your gifts. You won't take Him by surprise. God even understands your wordless prayers, when all you have are grunts or tears.

While being real and honest with God, remember to whom you are speaking. Be real while remaining respectful. Often, I begin my prayers with one or more of these verses, to show respect and honor:

Isaiah 6:3: *Holy, Holy, Holy, is the Lord of hosts, the whole earth is full of His glory.*

Isaiah 43:15: *I am the Lord, your Holy One, the Creator of Israel, your King.*

Exodus 15:11: *Who is like You among the gods, O Lord? Who is like You, majestic in holiness, awesome in praises, working wonders?*

1 Chronicles 29:11–13: *Yours, O Lord, is the greatness and the power and the glory and the victory and the majesty, indeed everything that is in the heavens and the earth; Yours is the dominion, O Lord, and You exalt Yourself as head over all. Both riches and honor come from You, and You rule over all, and in Your hand is power and might; and it lies in Your hand to make great and to strengthen everyone. Now therefore, our God, we thank You, and praise Your glorious name.*

What is the hardest part about exposing your true self to God?

Pray Intentionally and Specifically

Make time to pray. If we thought that someone's life depended on our prayer or that Jesus really would answer or that prayer is a powerful weapon, we'd all make prayer a top priority. Often, though, it's the last thing we do.

When and where do you pray?

God hears our prayers, even when we are multi-tasking — driving, for example. But when we're driving, we can be distracted by other drivers. We also need to pay attention to traffic lights and focus on what's around. So driving might not be the best time to pray.

Matthew 6:5 tells us, *When you pray, go into your inner room, close your door and pray to your Father who is in secret, and your Father who sees what is done in secret will reward you.*

Go into . . . find a private place, just for you and God. Is there a time and place you can pray in private, without distractions?

Then pray. Talk to God. Bring Him your burdens. Philippians 4:6 says, *Be anxious for nothing, but in everything by prayer and supplication with thanksgiving let your requests be made known to God.*

What burdens do you need to give to God?

Pray Continuously

First Thessalonians 5:17 tells us: *Pray without ceasing.* Paul doesn't mean that we never stop praying, but rather, our lifestyle would be marked by a continuous reflection of time spent with God:

- Humbly aware of His presence and greatness
- Thankful
- Priorities in right order
- Dependent on God

Colossians 1:9 says: *We have not ceased to pray for you and to ask that you may be filled with the knowledge of His will in all spiritual wisdom and understanding.*

Whom do you pray for regularly?

Whom do you ask to pray for you? Why did this person (or persons) make your list?

Do you ask God to give your friends knowledge and spiritual wisdom?

Pray with a Nonjudgmental Attitude

Sometimes when we're praying for loved ones, we inadvertently interject our desires for that person rather than ask God to reveal His purpose. Because of known sin, we might unintentionally pray critically. Following are examples of nonjudgmental prayers. Where there is a blank, fill in a name.

For children:

God, guide my young or adult children to hate what You hate and love what You love.

Pray 2 Timothy 1:7:

God has not given _____ *a Spirit of fear, but of power and of love, and of a sound mind.*

Give _____ *good judgment and right thinking."*

Pray 1 Chronicles 29:19, the words King David prayed for his son, Solomon, before he built the temple:

Give to [my son/daughter _____*] a perfect heart to keep Your commandments, Your testimonies, and Your statutes, and to do them all. [his/her purpose].*

Pray Colossians 1:7–14:

"God, I pray that _____ *will know Your specific plan for her/his life. May her/his conversation, character, and conduct, reveal obedience to You. I pray he/she will live in a manner worthy of Jesus Christ. I pray he/she will bear the fruit of the Spirit and influence the world one person at a time. I pray* _____ *will study the Bible, apply what it says, and grow closer to You every day. I pray he/she will recognize the connection between her decisions to obey and disobey You and the consequences or blessings that result. I pray* _____*will realize his/her helplessness and rely on Your strength. I pray she/he will remember to give thanks to You and to trust You. I pray that hardships will develop a deeper character. In Jesus' name, amen."*

Pray for your child/children's future husband or wife too.

For your husband:

Pray Ephesians 1:17–19: *Give to* _____ *a spirit of wisdom and of revelation in the knowledge of Him. I pray that the eyes of* _____*'s heart may be enlightened, so that* _____ *will know what is the hope of His calling, what are the riches of the glory of His inheritance in the saints, and what is the surpassing greatness of His power toward us who believe.*

Pray Psalm 119:18: *Open* _____
_____ *'s eyes, that [he] may behold wonderful things from Your law.*

For yourself:

Pray 2 Chronicles 15:7: *But you,* _____, *be strong and do not let your hands be weak, for your work will be rewarded.*

Pray Exodus 14:14: *The Lord will fight for you* _____ *while you keep silent.*

Pray Nehemiah 4:14: *Do not be afraid of them. Remember the Lord, great and awesome, and fight* _____ _____ *for your family and home.*

Pray Lamentations 2:19: *Pour out your heart like water,* _____, *for the life of your child[ren].*

Confess Your Sins

Read Psalm 66:18. When will God not hear a believer's prayer?

Recall Psalm 32:3–6. What did David do in response to his sin?

What did God do?

Read 1 John 1:9. To what person might we need to confess our sins?

After we confess to God, James urges us to confess our faults to
those affected by them and be _____
_____ (James 5: 16).

Is there anything hindering your prayers?

Pray with Praise and Thanksgiving

King David's prayers are an excellent example of heart felt, passionate
prayers. He ranted, questioned, and cried. But in predictable fashion,
he concluded most of his prayers with praise and thanksgiving. This
habit provides insight into David's relationship with God. He trusted
God. He believed God was worthy of being praised. Psalm 95:1–3
tells us, *O come, let us sing for joy to the LORD, let us shout joyfully to the
rock of our salvation. Let us come before His presence with thanksgiving, let
us shout joyfully to Him with psalms. For the LORD is a great God and a
great King above all gods.*

What can you thank God for today?

Remain Persistent and Steadfast

In the Luke 18:1–8 parable, Jesus doesn't say how many times
the widow approached the judge, but we can assume she came
more than once, often enough to irritate him. Jesus said to pray
with persistence. Don't give up. Keep coming back . . . until your
prayer is answered — with yes or no or wait or until God changes
your mind.

This widow didn't give up. Neither did Elijah.

Colossians 4:6 tells us: *Devote yourselves to prayer, keeping alert in
it with an attitude of thanksgiving.* And 1 Corinthians 15:58 says,
*Therefore, my beloved brethren, be steadfast, immovable, always abounding
in the work of the Lord, knowing that your toil is not in vain in the Lord.*

Is there anything you are praying for that would take a miracle?

What or whom have you given up on that you will begin earnestly praying for today?

Pray with Humility and Confidence

Humbly approach God. Hebrews 4:16 says: *Draw near with confidence to the throne of grace, so that we may receive mercy and find grace to help in time of need.*

And get a picture of sweetness: Psalm 116:2 says, *Because He has inclined His ear to me, therefore I shall call upon Him as long as I live.* The image of God bending low to hear sometimes invokes tears of joy.

In closing, write your name in the blank:

The effective prayer of _____ can accomplish much.

Prayer

God, help me know

- what to do.
- what to say.
- what to think.
- where to go.

For Reflection

What did God reveal about His character?

How have you been challenged in a specific area of your life?

How will you apply the passage to your daily routine?

How is your faith being strengthened?

X

It doesn't make sense that we can access God's most powerful weapon — prayer, but through prayer we become involved in God's plan and purpose and we shine forever.

X

Godly Friends Chime In

SAVANNAH says, "I'm okay with praying out loud, but my words seem weird to me sometimes when I hear them. I know this is a maturity thing, and I'm working on this. I'm more comfortable with writing out my prayers, so I like to keep a journal — and even draw my feelings."

CAROL jumps in. "I love, love, love this. Prayer for my family has helped me through some very troubled times. Years ago, I heard a Christian speaker say to pray for our children's future spouse. It has truly been a blessing to pray for a future spouse and personally know that the couple might build their home on Christ's love. Praise the Lord each of my children married a Christian, and now this is a prayer for each of my grandchildren."

LORI recalls a frightening experience. "As a police officer, it's my habit to call out to God for help, and the answer is needed, usually, within seconds. One time, I was called to a school with an armed gunman. I was told that the suspect was in a white vehicle but as I rounded the corner to the parking lot looking for the suspect, most of the vehicles were white. I remember saying out loud, 'Lord you've got to help me.' Suddenly over the radio came the words 'white jeep.' At the exact moment I needed, God answered my prayer for help."

Truths from James 5

- Be patient in suffering.
- Patience is possible when you focus on Jesus.
- Patience is a fruit of the Spirit.
- Store up everlasting treasure in heaven.
- Let your Christian integrity speak for you.
- Say *yes* or *no* and keep your word.
- A godly person with wealth can impact a lot of people.
- Wealth acquired wrongly or by an ungodly person will eventually end.
- Be impactful and productive while waiting for Christ's return.
- Sickness and death are part of the world in which we live.
- Jesus is our special treasure.
- Sometimes sickness is brought on by our choices.
- Pray for God's will when praying for the sick.
- Pray with confidence that God is good.
- Confession of sins brings spiritual healing.
- Prayer is a powerful weapon.
- Faith in God brings results.
- Help your Christian friends be accountable.
- A right relationship with God leads to obedience.
- Unconfessed sin creates distance between God and us.
- God sometimes heals physical, emotional, mental, and spiritual sickness.
- God gives grace to those He does not heal.
- Singing praise songs and hymns comforts us and honors God.
- Earnest prayer brings results.

Notes

When I first began writing this study, my husband was diagnosed with cancer. I finished writing in the middle of a pandemic, when COVID-19 spread throughout the world in 2020. How fitting that we end our study in the book of James on the topic of prayer.

Prayer sustains us in trials. Prayer, in fact, sustains our spiritual life. And during prayer, while we dwell in God's presence, we're focused, humbled, and hopeful. In desperation, we cast our burdens on Him. And in that place of peace, God meets us and satisfies our needs.

So there we have it. Stay in the presence of God, and you will shine on your journey. Our journey together through James ends now. But your personal journey with God is just beginning.

As a wrap, reflect on these questions:

Why do you think the content of James is considered a collection of proverbs?

What stood out the most to you from this book in the Bible?

What specifically will you apply to your personal life after five weeks of in-depth Bible study in James?

Comparatively speaking, how is your life different today than when you started this study?

How to Make a Decision for Jesus

The most important decision you will ever make has nothing to do with other people or anything on this earth. It doesn't even have anything to do with organized religion or a specific denomination. The most important decision you'll ever make is whether to have a personal relationship with Jesus Christ — a decision that will give you peace knowing you will spend eternity in heaven with God.

God's way is simple. We don't have to clean up our lives. We come to God as we are and He cleans us up.

God is holy and cannot be in the presence of sin. So out of His great love, compassion, and mercy for all people, God made a way for us to be in right relationship with Him. He sent His Son, Jesus, to pay the penalty for our sin. John 3:16 tells us: *God so loved the world, that He gave His only begotten Son, that whoever believes in Him shall not perish, but have eternal life.*

Admit you are a sinner. Ask God's forgiveness. Believe that Jesus died on the cross and three days later rose from death to life. Ask Him to be your Savior and take control of your life.

God has a beautiful plan and purpose for you.

You may find it easier to use this prayer: "God, I know I am a sinner. I'm sorry for my sins, and I ask Your forgiveness. I believe that You sent Your Son, Jesus Christ to pay the penalty for my sins and that He died and rose again. I invite You into my life. I give You control. Thank You for saving me. I know that I will spend eternity with You. In Jesus' name, amen."

If you prayed this prayer, please let someone know. You can email me at debpres@yahoo.com. Attend a Bible-believing church and cultivate your new, amazing relationship with God.

About the Author

Debbie Presnell, whose career has spanned more than three decades of teaching — from elementary school to higher education where she trained future teachers — is a member of Gardner-Webb University's Gallery of Distinguished Alumni; a multi-published author; a national speaker; and a Bible study teacher. She is the founder and director of Shine Camp for teenage girls, and Shine Conference for women. She is also the United States spokesperson for Mukti Mission in India, partnering with Mukti Mission US to bring hope, healing, and life to the women and children of India.

Debbie is called to inspire women and feels honored when God allows her the opportunity to share at women's events about His faithfulness. Debbie has authored four books: *Shine! Radiating the Love of God: A Bible Study Designed for Young Women in Middle School and High School*; *Shining Through the Psalms: A 150- Day Devotional Journey*; *Shine On! 30 Biblical Principles for Radiant Living*; and *Shining Through James: Living the Journey That Doesn't Make Sense*. Additionally, her articles have been published in the *Divine Moments* series. For the past 25 years, she has spoken at teacher conferences and universities where she shines the light on her favorite educational topic and the subject of an upcoming book: *The Inspirational Classroom*.

Debbie teaches a Bible study in her local church and is a regular speaker at the local women's prison. She shares devotions and brings inspirational messages on her Facebook page: ShineEveryDayNC.

She and her husband, Alan, have three adult children and two grandchildren. She enjoys camping, riding her bike, and helping coach a girl's running team. She loves both the mountains and the beach. When she's not busy writing or speaking, she serves as a substitute teacher in her local schools. But her best day is Sunday, when her entire family gathers for lunch. Visit her website at www.debbiepresnell.com. Email her at debpres@yahoo.com for information about having her speak to your group.

Shine Camp for Teens

Our mission is: equipping middle and high school girls with biblical principles that enable them to embrace their identity in Christ, strengthen their relationship with God, and impact their community.

If you are interested in hosting a Shine Camp at your church or in your community, contact Debbie Presnell at debpres@yahoo.com. You can also visit her website at www.debbiepresnell.com or visit Shine Camp on Facebook: SHINE Camp Black Mountain.

Shine Conference for Women

Debbie is passionate about sharing with women of all ages and denominations. For information on having Debbie speak at your women's event, contact her at debpres@yahoo.com or visit her website at www.debbiepresnell.com.

Mukti Mission US

Debbie serves as the United States spokesperson for Mukti Missions US — Bringing Hope, Healing, and Life to the women and children of India. A portion of the sales of all her books goes to support Mukti Mission. For more information or to donate, visit MuktiMission.us.

Other Books by Debbie Presnell

Shine! Radiating the Love of God: A Bible Study Designed For Young Women in Middle School and High School

Shining Through the Psalms: A 150 Day Devotional Journey

Shine On! 30 Biblical Principles for Radiant Living

I am most thankful to God for this journey.

I'm filled with gratitude for the woman who took part in my online James Bible Study group. You know who you are and I love you dearly.

I am in admiration of my husband's strength, and forever grateful for his support.

I'm so thankful for Terri. You are more than my publisher — you are my friend. I thank God that He divinely connected us way back at the Blue Ridge Mountains Christian Writer's Conference. Thank you for cheering me on.

I am also grateful for Denise — editor extraordinaire. Our conversations are enlightening and thought provoking. You have taught me so much.

I want to especially thank my godly friends who chimed in and shared their hearts and perspectives: Savannah, Meg, Jan, Carol, Sherry, Tamra, Eleanor, Judy, Cindy, Lorie, Gloria, Charla, Jamie, and Shelia. You made our journey through James so much better and I love you.

Shine On!

Endnotes

1. christiancourier.com/articles/305-lord-and-lord-whats-the-difference
2. biblestudytools.com/lexicons/greek/nas/doulos.html
3. https://www.blueletterbible.org/Comm/guzik_david/StudyGuide2017-Jam/Jam-1.cfm
4. http://biblehub.com/greek/1383.htm
5. http://www.studylight.org/dictionaries/ved/t/trial.html
6. http://www.biblestudytools.com/lexicons/greek/nas/peirasmos.html
7. https://biblehub.com/greek/5479.htm
8. https://www.merriam-webster.com/dictionary/count
9. https://biblehub.com/greek/5046.htm
10. Charles Spurgeon, *Morning and Evening* (Peabody: Hendrickson, 1995), 116.
11. Warren W. Wiersbe, *Be Mature* (Colorado Springs: David C. Cook, 2008) 111.
12. http://www.thefreedictionary.com/wisdom (and knowledge)
13. http://biblehub.com/greek/4678.htm
14. https://www.goodreads.com/quotes/29559
15. www.gotquestions.org/double-minded.html
16. www.merriam-webster.com/dictionary/wither
17. https://www.biblestudytools.com/lexicons/greek/nas/xeraino.html
18. https://www.encyclopedia.com/humanities/dictionaries-thesauruses-pictures-and-press-releases/tempt-0
19. https://www.mayoclinic.org/healthy-lifestyle/adult-health/in-depth/anger-management/art-20045434
20. Matthew Henry, *The Matthew Henry Commentary* (Grand Rapids: Zondervan, 1970), 1931.
21. *The Nelson's NKJV Study Bible*, notes on James 1:21
22. https://biblehub.com/greek/1387.htm
23. Dictionary.com
24. Webster's Online
25. Henry, *Commentary* 1932.
26. Wiersbe, *Be Mature* (David C. Cook, 2008), 77.
27. https://www.theatlantic.com/politics/archive/2012/05/poll-of-the-day-americans-attitutudes-about-sin/257550/
28. https://biblehub.com/hebrew/2398.htm
29. Albert Barnes, *Barnes' Notes on the Whole Bible*, "Commentary on James 4:4." https://www.studylight.org/commentaries/bnb/james-4.html, 1870.
30. Wiersbe, *Be Mature*, 77.
31. https://biblehub.com/topical/p/purify.htm
32. http://www.azquotes.com/author/11695-John_Piper/tag/obedience
33. biblehub.com/hebrew/8454.htm
34. https://www.merriam-webster.com/dictionary/friend
35. Patterson and Kelley, eds., *The Women's Evangelical Commentary — New Testament*, (Nashville: Broadman and Holman, 2006) 800.

36. Henry, *Commentary*, 1934

37. Ibid.

38. https://en.wikipedia.org/wiki/Sticks_and_Stones

39. *New King James Version, Personal Study Bible* (Nashville: Nelson Publishing, 1995)

40. merriam-webster.com/dictionary/restraint

41. https://biblehub.com/lexicon/ephesians/4-29.htm

42. Webster's online

43. http://www.christianquotes.info/quotes-by-topic/quotes-about-gossip/#ixzz4Czhow1uf

44. https://biblehub.com/greek/diaboloi_1228.htm

45. https://www.gotquestions.org/double-minded.html

46. https://www.desiringgod.org/articles/what-does-it-mean-to-bless-god

47. http://www.thefreedictionary.com/wisdom/knowledge

48. Wiersbe, *Be Mature* 115-119

49. https://www.biblestudytools.com/lexicons/greek/nas/moichalis.html

50. https://www.merriam-webster.com/dictionary/jealous

51. http://www.desiringgod.org/messages/do-not-love-the-world

52. Wiersbe, *Be Mature*,132

53. lexico.com/en/definition/proud

54. merriam-webster.com/dictionary/humility

55. https://www.lexico.com/en/definition/grace

56. Wiersbe, *Be Mature*, 132.

57. https://biblehub.com/commentaries/psalms/51-17.htm

58. Barnes, *Barnes' Notes on the New Testament,* "Commentary on Psalms, (Grand Rapids" Kregel), 34:18

59. https://biblehub.com/greek/2636.htm

60. https://biblehub.com/commentaries/2_timothy/4-2.htm

61. Ibid.

62. vocabulary.com/dictionary/confrontation

63. merriam-webster.com/dictionary/confrontation

64. biblestudytools.com/lexicons/greek/nas/parakaleo.html

65. https://johndabell.com/2019/06/18/teachers-make-35000-decisions-a-day/

66. https://www.merriam-webster.com/dictionary/omission

67. merriam-webster.com/dictionary/treasure

68. www.merriam-webster.com/thesaurus/patience

69. biblestudytools.com/lexicons/hebrew/nas/qavah.html

70. Charles Stanley, *In Touch Magazine,* https://808bo.com/2015/03/06/

71. www.vocabulary.com/dictionary/oath

72. Wiersbe, *Be Mature*, 169.

73. Henry, *Commentary*, 1937-1938

74. www.desiringgod.org/interviews/should-christians-swear-on-the-bible

75. Ibid.

76. Webster's Dictionary

77. biblestudytools.com/lexicons/greek/nas/astheneo.html

78. www.ncbi.nlm.nih.gov/pmc/articles/PMC5876976/--

79. www.nimh.nih.gov/health/statistics/mental-illness.shtml

80. www.heart.org/en/health-topics/cardiomyopathy/what-is-cardiomyopathy-in-adults/is-broken-heart-syndrome-real

81. biblehub.com/greek/1637.htm

82. biblehub.com/lexicon/psalms/147-3.htm

83. Ibid.

84. https://www.merriam-webster.com/dictionary/fervent